. THE .
High Wycombe Advertiser

Distributed gratis throughout the town.

No. 30.　　　　　WEDNESDAY, SEPT. 23, 1896.　　　　　GRATIS.

L.29

YESTERDAY'S TOWN: WYCOMBE

Horse 'bus outside Little Market House c1900.

High Street 1864.

YESTERDAY'S TOWN:
WYCOMBE

BY

IVAN G. SPARKES

BARRACUDA BOOKS LIMITED
BUCKINGHAM, ENGLAND
MCMLXXXIII

PUBLISHED BY BARRACUDA BOOKS LIMITED
BUCKINGHAM, ENGLAND
AND PRINTED BY
BURGESS & SON (ABINGDON) LIMITED
ABINGDON, ENGLAND

BOUND BY
J.W. BRAITHWAITE & SON LIMITED
WOLVERHAMPTON, ENGLAND

JACKET PRINTED BY
CHENEY & SONS LIMITED
BEDFORD, ENGLAND

PHOTO LITHOGRAPHY BY
BICESTER PHOTO LITHO LIMITED
BICESTER, ENGLAND

DISPLAY SET IN TIMES
AND TEXT SET IN 12/13 TIMES ROMAN BY
BEDFORDSHIRE GRAPHICS LIMITED
BEDFORD, ENGLAND

ISBN 0 86023 157 7

CONTENTS

INTRODUCTION

When writing *The Book of Wycombe* some years ago, I attempted to cover the history of this town from prehistory through to the 20th century. This time, I am not quite so ambitious, limiting my period from 1830 to 1930. Even so, this was a time of great change, for the country, in the field of politics, local government and social life. I have found it fascinating to draw on the contemporary reminiscences which abound in the *Bucks Free Press* from its inception in 1856, and in the work of others, writing as contemporaries of the time. In consequence, this book has become something less of a history book, than a pot pourri of episodes which, I hope, illustrate the lives of our predecessors in High Wycombe. I would thank all those who have drawn to my attention photographs etc, which I have been able to copy and add to the collection. Indeed, as the years go by, it seems that more and more old photographs and postcards keep coming to light!

June 1983   I.G. Sparkes

WEST WYCOMBE.

WEST WYCOMBE SCHOOL BOARD.—A meeting of the Board was held on Monday, Present. Mr. J. Crook in the chair, and Messrs. Martin, Harman, and Bristow. The treasurer's account showed a balance in favour of the Board of £300 14s. 10d., and cheques were drawn for the usual salaries of the officers.—A letter was read from the master of Booker School, stating that H.M. Inspector had recently visited and reported as follows. "I find the babies class is still regular teacher. The grant ticle may have to be reduced f thing is allowed to continue." was of opinion that the staff it, and requested the clerk to ector at Wycombe on the 15th scertain what was really re- was ordered that tenders be coal and coke for the next he Board.

Births, Marriages, and Deaths.

DEATHS.

BIRCH.—At Lower Gordon-road, on October 1st, Ivy Mary Birch, aged 6 months.

BUSBY.—At 122, Desborough-road, on September 29th, William Arthur Busby, aged 18 days.

COX.—At Spread Eagle-yard, on October 2nd, Elizabeth Cox, aged 67 years.

GRAY.—At Copy Ground-lane, on October 2nd, Frederick Gray, aged 3 months.

KEEN.—At 32, Oxford-road, on September 29th, Charles Walter Keen, aged 10 months.

PARKER.—At 8, Collins-row, on September 29th, James Parker, age 11 months.

SAWYER.—At Little Kingshill, on October 3rd, Bertha Sawyer, aged 15 months.

SUMMERFIELD.—At the Marsh, Chepping Wycombe, on October 1st, Millicent Fanny Summerfield, aged 20 months.

ROGERS.—At Green-street, on October 4th, Harry Rogers, aged 20 years.

THE CHINESE TROUBLE.

Confirmatory of yesterday's report, the officials at the Chinese Legation, state, says the Central News, that complete order is restored in Pekin. They are, however, without official information as to the Emperor's health.

THE RAILWAY SERVANTS' CONGRESS.

At the meeting of the Congress at Leeds to-day the resolution moved yesterday, condemning the recent train-wrecking attempts, was unanimously confirmed. A committee was also appointed to enquire into the charges against Mr. Garrity, the Assistant Secretary, and it was decided to supply him with every information to enable him to prepare his defence.

LOCAL GOVERNMENT INQUIRY.

Some time ago the Town Council of ...combe applied to the Local Government Board for sanction to borrow £1,320 ...works of sewage and sewage disposal, £580 for the construction of a new ...ge and road. In accordance with the ...om of the Board a local enquiry was ... at the Town Hall on Tuesday morning by Major-General H. D. Crozier, R.A. ...re were present the Mayor (Mr. D. ...rke), Ald. Hunt (Chairman of the ...lic Works Committee), Councillors ...R. Peace, G. W. Deacon, and A. J. ...sby, Mr. A. J. Clarke (Town Clerk), ...r. Bradshaw (Borough Medical Officer of Health), Mr. T. J. Rushbrook (Borough Surveyor), and Mr. Isaac Bonnett, Inspector representing the Thames Conservancy.—The Town Clerk read the notice convening the meeting, &c., and in reply to the questions by the inspector said the population of the Borough at the last census was 13,435. That was estimated to have increased to between 15,000 and 16,000. The assessable value was £32,885. The outstanding loans were stated to be £21,523. The amount of £1,328 was made up of £1,209 for extra expenditure incurred by the authority in carrying out the work at the sewage outfall, which was in ...
the present time. The £1·...
...extend... the sewer ...
and along Priory-road ...
of the plans the ...
opinion, that
sufficient ...

Wycombe Mail 5 October 1898

YESTERDAY'S TOWN

ABOVE: Frogmore, looking across to Hearn's Corner c1910;
BELOW: Frogmore — North side c1920.

ABOVE LEFT: Frogmore in the snow 1908; RIGHT: Frogmore with pseudo-Tudor cinema front c1930; BELOW: Frogmore with re-modelled cinema front c1940.

10

ABOVE: Demolition of the Frogmore Fountain in the Second World
War; BELOW: High Street, 1901; the return of troops from the Boer
War.

ABOVE: Bucks Militia returned from Boer War 1901; and BELOW:
St Mary Street Arch for men of Bucks Yeomanry returned from the
Boer War 1901.

ABOVE: Royal Bucks Hussars in Queen Victoria Road 1914;
LEFT: Mafeking Night in the High Street; ABOVE RIGHT: Liberal
Club in High Street, with access to Majestic on right c1930; BELOW
RIGHT: High Street with Davenport Vernon's on corner c1920.

ABOVE: Band Contest, High Street c1920; BELOW: Military Band
in Queen Victoria Road 1931.

ABOVE LEFT: High Wycombe at night;
ABOVE RIGHT: fire in Crendon Street 1906;
BELOW: interior of Christchurch, Crendon
Street.

ABOVE: High Street and Crendon Lane as alterations take place c1930; CENTRE: Easton Street Parade, July 1914; BELOW LEFT: corner of Crendon Lane and Easton Street c1920; BELOW RIGHT: Wright's Dairy, Easton Street.

ABOVE: Easton Street c1890; CENTRE: Mr Hadows' Boys School
1908; BELOW: Railway Viaduct over Temple End c1910.

A Mass Meeting
OF THE
CHAIRMAKERS
OF WYCOMBE
WILL BE HELD IN
THE RYE,
ON
Saturday Evening Next.

To consider the Sweating Practices
introduced into Wycombe Trade, and
also the conduct of Messrs. Birch at the
present time.   To be Addressed by

MR. TOM WALKER
(Of the Alliance Cabinet Makers' Association.)

AND OTHERS.

TO COMMENCE AT 6 P.M. SHARP.

ABOVE: Beechwoods around High Wycombe; BELOW
LEFT: chair factory of W. Woodbridge, Temple c1880;
BELOW RIGHT: poster for mass meeting of
chairmakers.

18

ABOVE: Henry Goodearl's factory, West End Road 1886;
BELOW: workers of 'Bobbies' of Slater Street in the 1930s.

19

ABOVE: High Wycombe lockout pickets 1914; BELOW: munition
workers in First World War.

ABOVE: C.C. Hugo munition workers 1917; BELOW: Dexter and
Co munition workers, First World War.

LOYAL BOROUGH

The 1830s and 1840s were a period of great change in both the political and administrative life of the town. Not only did the 1832 Parliamentary Reform Act dramatically alter the way in which our Members of Parliament were elected, but other legislation, such as the Catholic Emancipation Act and the Corn Laws, affected strongly-held religious views and involved the staple trade of the Market Town. In addition to all this, in 1835 came the final indignity of an investigation into the way in which the Borough was run, involving a close look at the Common Council itself, its traditions and powers.

We were still in the reign of William IV, and High Wycombe was a market town of some 6,000 inhabitants (census 1831: 6,299) lying along the length of the Wye Valley, but confined to quite a small area up each side of the valley itself. The boundaries stretched from just above the present railway station, continuing west to Temple Farm at Temple End, which is just beyond Frogmore on the Hughenden Road, then on the Oxford Road south of the river to just beyond Bridge Street, when it turned sharply south to Desborough Road, then doubled back to Wycombe Abbey to run through the middle of the Dyke until it turned across the Rye to Rye Mill, and back to Pann Mill, then north and east to meet up back at the railway station. The Manor House at Bassetbury was in the hands of Sir John Dashwood-King of West Wycombe, who was one of the Members of Parliament for High Wycombe, while the patronage of the other seat in the Commons was in the control of the Carrington family, who owned Wycombe Abbey.

The nature of trade in the town is indicated by the several directories published at the time, and Pigot's 1830 directory is a good example. It shows us craftsmen in such lost trades as basketmaking, a family consisting of James, Robert and William Youens of Oxford Street and Paul's Row, or the three Hulls, Isaac, John and Joseph of Market Place and Paul's Row who were braziers and tinmen. There were also fellmongers, hatters, lace dealers and even parchment makers, and of course there were plenty of papermakers and chair makers. The many inns in the town were supplied by the two brewers, William Huntley of The Canal (which was Frogmore) and Robert Wheeler of High Street, whose brewery stood roughly to the west of Queen Victoria Road, stretching from the present firm of Connells, down to the end of the Post Office yard.

There were also five maltsters in the town who helped to assuage the thirst of local drinkers. Other long-standing names included John Young, the rope-maker, William T. Butler, the printer and Joseph Sheriff, one of the nineteen bakers in the town.

Some of the streets had been paved earlier in 1810, when the cobblestones were removed and replaced with setts from Denner Hill. One or two examples of the old cobbled paving still remain, noticeably on the parking areas in front of the Falcon in the Cornmarket, and at the entrance to the Church. The flagstones under the Little Market House were replaced in the 1840s with sandstone setts, and the original ones

were taken up and used to pave the area under the Guildhall. An attempt to light the streets by gas had been made in 1833, but it was not until the Gas Works were built in 1848 that this became feasible.

The policing of the town was done by watchmen at night, who acted under the supervision of Robert Eades, who kept the gaol in Newlands. The town was divided into three 'beats' for surveillance:

Beat No 1 or High Street: down High Street and Eastern Street to the end of the Borough, up Billy's Alley along Town Field, examining Crendon Lane by the Way through the Churchyard to the Station House.

Beat No 2 or Paul's Row Beat: through Church Street, round the Canal, through Kings Head Yard, return through Bull Lane or Queens Square along White Hart Street by Pauls Row to the southern end of Saint Mary Street, and back by Crown Lane to the Station House.

Beat No 3 or Newland Beat: over Newland Bridge, past the Alms Houses, examine Millers rent, on by Watsons to Long Row, back by the gaol to Morecrafts Meadow as far as the end of the Borough, return by the Catherine Wheel, occasionally examining Bird Cage Walk.

According to their regulations, the policemen 'are not to enter into any public house or beer shop, etc., except for the purpose of removing disorderly persons, or complaining of such houses remaining open beyond the lawful hours, which cases they are to report to the superintendent at his next visit'. The beer in those days would have been somewhat more potent than that available now, and the statutory hours of opening rather longer. The spirits of the people almost matched the spirits, or at least the liquor available, at the time of the elections. In one particular case on record, the election of Sir J. Dashwood-King and Sir Thomas Baring in 1830, the entertainment and flowing beer were quite amazing, with 27 barrels of 60 gallons each of beer being distributed by 27 publicans to the people of Chepping Wycombe as they gathered to the hustings. The chair which was painted by Charles Skull stayed for some years at the White Hart, but now stands more suitably in Hughenden Manor, once the home of Benjamin Disraeli.

Many people in the town were in favour of political reform, as this could radically affect their ability to vote in the elections, both municipal and parliamentary. For, up to the early 1830s, although most of the shopkeepers paid Borough rates, poor rates, and a Church rate to the Parish Vestry, they were not necessarily Burgesses or able to have much say in local and national political matters.

Not that there were many projects under way at the time, as the income of the Borough was small. This meant that not only could little new be done in the town in the way of improvements, but also that some cuts in current spending might be necessary. The Town Crier and Beadle, who formerly had 10 shillings weekly was cut in 1833 to £10 per annum, and the two night watchmen had their wages cut from 10 shillings and sixpence weekly to 8 shillings in the summer and 10s 6d in the winter, and also warned that their uniforms, which were supplied by the Council, would have to last much longer. The problems of Borough finances were further highlighted by the warring factions within the town. The Council, using the

precedents of earlier Charters, created new burgesses to enable them to control parliamentary voting and, with the growing size of High Wycombe, became unrepresentative of the town as a whole.

At this point parliamentary reforms began to make themselves felt. The 'Wycombe Society of Friends of Rational and Efficient Reform' was set up, and a petition sent to Parliament in February 1831. The Reform Bill was introduced into the Commons in March 1831, which allowed for two standing MPs for the town, but extended the franchise to include the 'foreigns'. Of the two Members of Parliament in office, Sir Thomas Baring was for the Bill, but Sir John Dashwood-King was against it. In October 1831, the House of Lords rejected the Bill, and the local population was outraged. The shops were closed in High Wycombe, and shutters put up against the expected riots. The town that day watched an effigy of Lord Wharncliffe hanged from the lamp bracket outside the Guildhall, and another effigy, that of Lord Carrington of Wycombe Abbey, the 'Abbot' as he was called, was paraded around the streets and burnt in St Mary Street onto which his estate gates opened.

But all was well in May 1832 for, when the Duke of Wellington failed to form a government, Lord Grey returned, to push through the Reform Bill. And here in Wycombe, the town rejoiced, with the bell-ringers manning their bells with a will, and the town band marching around the streets. It was on the wave of this enthusiasm that Benjamin Disraeli decided to stand for Parliament, to use his words, 'as a reformer', and within the town itself a deputation led by the chairmaker family of Treachers presented to the Common Council a memorial from the new voters under the Reform Act, 'requesting the Mayor, Bailiffs, and Burgesses to elect Benjamin Disraeli, esquire to represent this Borough'. Unfortunately for both Disraeli and the Treachers, Colonel Grey, son of the Prime Minister himself, presented himself as a candidate for High Wycombe, sponsored by Lord Carrington; so Disraeli failed. As he commented later, according to a street rhyme:-

> 'I really can't imagine why,
> With my confessed ability,
> From the Ungrateful Tories, I
> Get nothing but civility.'

The job of a Member of Parliament in High Wycombe was no sinecure, as the electors, in particular the Common Council, expected him to lay any petition they would wish to bring to Her Majesty's attention, before the Palace or Parliament. The Town was anti-Catholic in the past, so they protested against any relief given to Catholics in the new Catholic Emancipation Bill, which was then going through Parliament. They also petitioned against the Income Tax proposals of 1842: 'Your petitioners cannot refrain from expressing to your Ladyship their abhorance of such a tax, when past experience have fully proved, under the semblance of impartiality, to be essentially must unjust and oppressive'. This Bill was passed in June 1842, allowing for a general tax of 7d on income and property. But perhaps the petition which most fully expressed their feelings of loyalty to the Crown, was that of 17 June 1840, following the attempted assassination of the Queen: . . . 'We your Majesty's

dutiful and Loyal Subjects, approach your Majesty's Throne with hearts filled with gratitude to Almighty God for his preservation of the lives of your Majesty and your August Consort . . . we reflect with a horror only equalled by our indignation that a wretch should exist under the form of an Englishman who would put in peril a life so dear to the nation as that of your Majesty'.

Royalty had a strong connection with the Borough and, as Princess Victoria, before succeeding to the throne, passed through Wycombe on 9 November 1832, the town felt a personal commitment to her. The Princess travelled with her mother, the Duchess of Kent, and stopped at the Red Lion to change horses. There was also a close relationship between Lord Carrington and HRH Prince of Wales, which was the reason for several Royal visits to the town. In 1884 the Prince and Princess of Wales agreed to accept a gift of two Wycombe chairs. When Queen Victoria visited Disraeli at Hughenden Manor in 1877, she stopped to admire the chair manufacturers' Arch of Chairs at the Guildhall.

However servile the Corporation might sound from the tone of their petitions to the Queen, and however personal their loyalty and love for the Royal family, they never went so far as to forget the overwhelming importance of High Wycombe in their own eyes.

When the way in which the country was being run did not meet with their general approval, they had no hesitation, such as in October 1841, in sending yet another petition to the Queen, sadly pointing out that 'We had hoped that under divine providence, your Majesty's reign would have been blessed with Peace abroad, Plenty at home, but we had heard with grief of great and extensive distress in the Kingdom. We rely on your Majesty's love for your faithful and devoted people for the adoption of such measures as shall remove the causes of the present distress and fill with joy and gratitude the hearts of your Majesty's subjects'.

LIST OF MAYORS
1855 — 1910

	Elected
Thomas Wheeler	1855
William Henry Hayden	1856
Alfred Lane, junr.	1857
Buckmaster Joseph Tuck	1858
Robert Wheeler	1859
Robert Wheeler	1860
Ralph Lansdale	1861
Thomas Wheeler	1862
Joseph Hunt	1863
Purton Weston	1864
Charles Strange	1865
Robert Wheeler	1866
John Turner	1867
Thomas Wheeler	1867
John Turner	1868
William Henry Hayden	1869
John Parker, junr.	1870
Joseph Hunt	1871
Francis Wheeler	1872
Thomas Gilbert	1873
Thomas Wheeler	1874
William Vincent Baines	1875
George Wheeler	1876
William Phillips	1877
James George Peace	1878
(Since the Extension of the Borough in 1880)	
William Henry Hayden	1879
Thomas Wheeler JP	1880
Thomas Wheeler JP	1881
Arthur Vernon JP	1882
Arthur Vernon JP	1883
Aubrey Brook Weston	1884
George Wheeler	1885
George Wheeler	1886
William Phillips JP	1887
William Phillips JP	1888
Thomas Glenister JP	1889
Thomas Glenister JP	1890
Arthur Vernon JP	1891
Charles Harman Hunt	1892
Charles Thomas Baines	1893
Richard Goodearl JP	1894
John Busby JP	1895
Philip John Rutland JP	1896
Daniel Clarke CA JP	1897
Charles William Deacon JP	1898
Robert Davenport Vernon JP	1899
Walter Birch JP	1900
(Since the extension of the Borough in 1901)	
Walter Birch JP	1901
Daniel Clarke CA JP	1902
Daniel Clarke CA JP	1903
Charles Henry Elsom	1904
Arthur Vernon JP.	1905
Arthur Vernon JP	1906
Robert Samuel Wood	1907
William Wharton JP	1908
Walter Birch JP	1909
Henry Joliffe Cox	1910

ABOVE: Chepping Wycombe Council 1879/80 at Dr Hayden's
House, Frogmore; BELOW: Chepping Wycombe Borough Council
in the Guildhall 1928.

ABOVE: Mayor's procession c1912 with Dame Frances Dove, the
first woman Councillor; BELOW: Borough Council outing on the
Thames c1900.

TOP ROW, LEFT TO RIGHT: Alderman A. Vernon JP Mayor 1882/3, 1883/4, 1891/2, 1905/6, 1906/7; Daniel Clarke, Town Clerk then Mayor 1902/3, 1903/4; Alderman C.H. Hunt, Mayor 1892/3; MIDDLE ROW, LEFT TO RIGHT: Councillor Brocklehurst, Mayor 1935/6; Alderman W.R. Butler, Mayor 1924/5; P.C. Raffety ; BOTTOM ROW, LEFT TO RIGHT: George Wheeler, Mayor 1876/7, 1885/6, 1886/7; Alderman Richard T. Graefe, Mayor 1911/12, 1912/13, 1913/14; Thomas Glenister, Mayor 1889/90, 1890/91.

TOP ROW, LEFT TO RIGHT: William Rose Mayor 1848/9;
Robert Davenport Vernon, Mayor 1899/1900; Robert Wheeler
Senior, Mayor, 1812/13, 1819/20, 1825/6, 1832/3, 1834/5, 1835/
6, 1837/8,, 1846/7, 1852/3; LEFT: John Gomme, Mayor, 1913/4,
1914/5, 1915/6; CENTRE LEFT: Alderman James George Peace,
Mayor 1878/9; RIGHT: Owen Haines, Mayor, 1917/8, 1918/9;
BELOW LEFT: Aleck Stacey, Mayor 1928/9, 1929/30; RIGHT:
Ralph Janes, Mayor 1925/6, 1926/7.

TOP ROW, LEFT TO RIGHT: C.T. Baines, Mayor 1893/4; Mr
Bond, Station master 1894; Mr F. Westfield, Postmaster 1894;
BELOW, LEFT TO RIGHT: Head Constable Sparling, 1894; Dr
Fleck; Lord Curzon MP; OPPOSITE ABOVE RIGHT: Jubilee
1887, invitation to dinner at Town Hall, May 27, 1887; LEFT: lines
on the visit of HRH Prince of Wales 1882; RIGHT: Jubilee 1887,
menu card for Jubilee dinner, 22 June, 1887; BELOW: rubbing of
medal commemorating the death of Earl of Beaconsfield 1881.

LINES ON THE VISIT OF
H. R. H. THE PRINCE OF WALES
TO WYCOMBE, 18TH MAY, 1882.

Hark, the joyous bells are pealing,
  Merrily indeed they ring,
Gladly giving hearty greeting,
  Unto England's future king.

Now he comes, a guest to honour
  One to Wycombe people dear,
Loyally will he receive him,
  And be glad to see him here.

Once within that stately mansion,
  Though a Prince he'll surely find,
There, an English heart that's ready,
  Noble, manly, true and kind.

Ready, waiting to receive him,
  In a true and princely way,
Where he'll have a hearty welcome,
  Welcome as the flowers in May.

Let this day be long remembered,
  In the spring time of the year,
When all nature seems rejoicing,
  And the sky is bright and clear.

When the birds are gaily singing,
  And the leaves are fresh and green,
Nature clad in all its beauty,
  Is it not a charming scene ?

Then it is that Wycombe Abbey,
  Opens wide its lordly hall,
And the future king of England,
  Comes obedient to its call.

Comes to pay a promised visit,
  In a friendly kind of way,
May this pleasant happy meeting
  Be renewed some future day.

May our Prince thro' life be happy,
  Crowned with blessings from above,
And His Consort " England's Princess,"
  Who has gained a nation's love.

May the noble lord of Wycombe,
  Yet be spared to entertain,
With his estimable lady,
  England's future king again.

H. B.

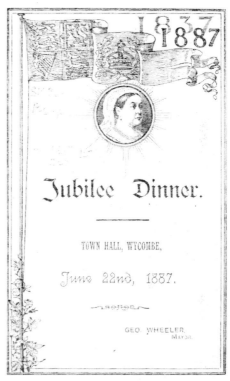

31

PLANTING THE HUGHENDEN TREE.

IGH is Aylesbury's fame for her dairies,
  High is Aylesbury's fame for her ducks,
But High-Wycombe enjoys greater glory,
  The most-favoured borough in Bucks!
The renown of a Hughenden Manor,
  The luck of a Beaconsfield nigh,
To shed on her doings and dwellers
  The light from an Asian sky.

One industry that favoured borough
  Has based on her fair beechen woods,
The making of chairs, pails, and platters,
  And all sorts of "turnery" goods.
All fashions of backs and of bottoms,
  Of arms and of legs—four by four—
That from kitchen and bed-room ascending,
  To Windsor, in apogee, soar.

At length to that neat little borough
  Where so many Windsors they frame,
In this blessèd month of December
  The Lady of Windsor there came!
Victoria, *in propriâ personâ*,
  To Hughenden Manor drove o'er,
With Hughenden's Lord to take luncheon,—
  A grace deigned few subjects before.

Sore travailed the brains of the borough,
  Of Aldermen, Town-Clerk, and Mayor!
Who shall tell of the meetings and motions,
  And appeals—as of right—to the Chair?
How should High Wycombe rise to its highest,
  Its loyal invention to show,
In building an archway triumphal,
  For the Queen underneath it to go!

Christmas evergreens, holly and laurel,
  Were there, but such archways were stale;
Mere battens, distemper, and canvas,
  Were all in the common-place pale;
Till 'twas planned—who proposed it we know not,
  His blushes posterity spares—
Both her trade and her loyalty Wycombe,
  Should proclaim in an archway of chairs!

Of all arches ever passed under
  By Royal Procession before,
Never arch displayed loyalty greater,
  And none e'er struck Royalty more.
There was but one feature a-wanting,
  As a crown of the arch in the air,
Had Lord Beaconsfield posed, emblematic,
  A-poising a neat Windsor chair!

Pass we o'er the address and the bouquet,
  And the Bucks Volunteers on the green,
And drive on to Hughenden Manor,
  Where its honoured Lord welcomes his Queen,
His Empress—to whom he has added
  A title was ne'er Queen's before,
And now, his full cup over-brimming,
  As his guest sees her darkening his door!

Did the Czar in far Bucharest shiver?
  Did Gortschakoff thrill with a dread?
Did the Sultan in Stamboul feel less of
  The thorns where he pillows his head?'
As from luncheon in Hughenden Manor
  The Queen and my radiant Lord B.
Walked out to the lawn, and proceeded
  To plant a memorial tree!

Oh, what was the tree my Lord ordered,—
  Or was it the Queen that bespoke?
Was it poplar, or alder, or laurel?—
  ! It could scarcely have been British Oak.
Or a tree of some Asian order,
  Till now to our *Silva* unknown,
From a Hebrew root shot up in no time,
  With a coronet-flower, newly blown?

Was 't a growth from the islands Pacific,
  Or a shoot from some battle-fed seed,
With promise of *Sang-de-Bœuf* blossoms,
  And wood good for gun-stocks at need?
Whatever the tree that was planted
  At Hughenden Manor that day,
To the trees our Queen plants 'tis the usage
  That we should have something to say.

There's war on Bulgarian mountains,
  And war in Armenian plains,
But to England, that watches the battles,
  Thank God! blessèd peace still remains;
And ere she takes hand from the ploughshare
  And loom to lay hand to the sword,
Be assured she will well weigh the reason,
  With due faith in her Queen and my Lord.

Cartoon and poem — planting the Hughenden Tree.

Lord Carrington, taken in Sydney in 1888.

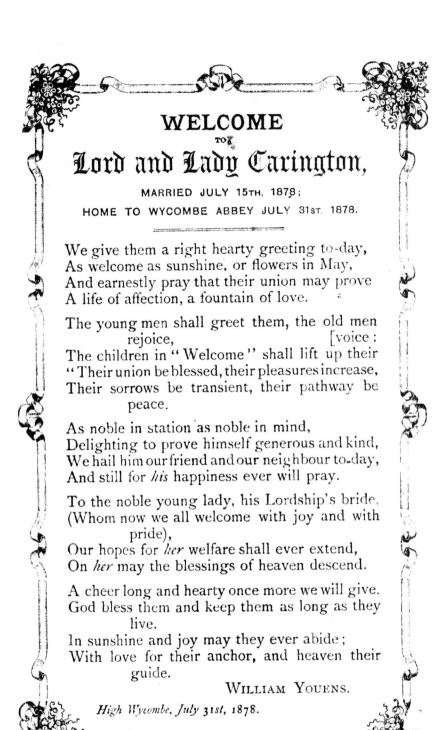

WELCOME
TO
Lord and Lady Carington,

MARRIED JULY 15TH, 1878;

HOME TO WYCOMBE ABBEY JULY 31ST, 1878.

We give them a right hearty greeting to-day,
As welcome as sunshine, or flowers in May,
And earnestly pray that their union may prove
A life of affection, a fountain of love.

The young men shall greet them, the old men
rejoice, [voice:
The children in "Welcome" shall lift up their
"Their union be blessed, their pleasures increase,
Their sorrows be transient, their pathway be
peace.

As noble in station as noble in mind,
Delighting to prove himself generous and kind,
We hail him our friend and our neighbour to-day,
And still for *his* happiness ever will pray.

To the noble young lady, his Lordship's bride,
(Whom now we all welcome with joy and with
pride),
Our hopes for *her* welfare shall ever extend,
On *her* may the blessings of heaven descend.

A cheer long and hearty once more we will give.
God bless them and keep them as long as they
live.
In sunshine and joy may they ever abide;
With love for their anchor, and heaven their
guide.

WILLIAM YOUENS.

High Wycombe, July 31st, 1878.

Butler, Printer, Wycombe.

Welcome poem for Lord and Lady Carrington, 1878.

HIGH WYCOMBE.

Arrangements for
RECEPTION
OF
LORD & LADY CARINGTON
JULY 31st, 1878.

THE COMMITTEE have endeavoured to ascertain the views and wishes of Lord Carington, and with his Lordship's concurrence have made the following arrangements, which it is hoped the public will assist in carrying out.

His Lordship is expected to arrive by the train which reaches High Wycombe at 2.33 p.m. The public bodies and tenantry will meet His Lordship at the Railway Station and form a procession, preceded by the Band, to a space reserved for the purpose in front of the Red Lion Hotel, High Street, where the several Addresses will be presented to LORD AND LADY CARINGTON, After which the Procession will proceed to the Abbey.

It is expected that the Horses will be taken from the Carriage **after the Addresses have been presented and received,** and the Carriage will be drawn to the Abbey by Ropes.

Fireworks in the Rye at 9.15 p.m.

BUTLER, PRINTER, WYCOMBE.

Poster regarding reception of Lord and Lady Carrington 1878.

VOTE FOR CARINGTON,

THE LIBERAL CANDIDATE.

A NEW ELECTION SONG.

Air.---"Dare to be a Daniel."

Rise, friends, rise, there's work to do
  Up and down the land,
Work which needs men good and true,
  And brave in heart and hand.

Chorus.—Dare to be a Liberal,
    Dare your rights to claim,
    Dare to fight for truth and right,
    And leave a noble name.

Many wrongs you've long endured
  Cutting to the core,
But these wrongs may now be cured
  And ne'er afflict you more.

    Chorus.—Dare to be a Liberal.

Many Tories puff'd with pride
  Raise their hands on high,
All your claims as men, deride,
  And frowning pass you by.

    Chorus.—Dare to be a Liberal.

Show these Tories you are men,
  Men who dare to be
Heroes in a noble cause,
  Assured of victory.

    Chorus—Dare to be a Liberal.

Let them see your hearts are true,
  Show them you can fight,
Pierce the Tory armour through,
  And put them all to flight.

    Chorus.—Dare to be a Liberal.

Raise the Liberal banner high
  Tory hosts withstand ;
"Gladstone" be our rallying cry
  That name so great and grand.

    Chorus—Dare to be a Liberal.

Buckingham.   T. Baker, Jun.

Printed and Published by George Potter, 14, Fetter Lane, London.

Vote for Carrington — election song.

AN ACROSTIC.

—••◦✕◦••—

C an feeble words of mine, or pen express

H ow much beloved is he I now address—

A n Englishman in very heart and soul,

R eady and true as " needle to the pole,"

L ives not for self, has no such mean desire—

E ach poorer neighbour loves its country squire,

S o lives the man whose actions we admire.

R ejoice we do that Wycombe still can boast

O f Wycombe Abbey and its noble host.

B eautiful home, by nature richly blessed,

E 'en long may it, by him be still possess'd

R ecalling oft those happy days of joy,

T rue bliss to him who knew thee from a boy.

C hill blasts of trouble will at times come o'er,

A nd make us tremble on this earthly shore ;

R eal happiness alone we only find

R ewards the man who is to others kind.

I n this no man a nobler part can play,

N one but will gladly join me when I say—

G od bless his Lady and his children dear,

T o cheer his heart, and make him happy here ;

O may no evil thee or thine betide,

N or fear it will, if God be still thy guide.

H. BENNETT.

OLD JOHNNY MILLS IN TROUBLE !!

1.

Oh ! crikey, John, why here's a go !
Why Billy Carington, you know,
Is going to have a jolly row
Right down the River Wick.

2.

As sure as two and two make four,
He's gaining favor more and more :
They say he's right up to the door—
He is a jolly brick !

3.

Although you paid the money down
To pave the streets in Wycombe Town ;
And Punch said " got you great renown "—
It will not save you now.

4.

Though councillors in room there were,
They did the thing unjust, unfair :
It did with partial party glare—
And you will know it now.

5.

The grunting, growling—it is strong,
Your friends they did do very wrong,
They thought themselves so very strong—
And thus comes up the row.

6

Now Billy is both strong and tall,
He pulls his oars without a fall,
He gets along with great and small,
And he will win the race.

7.

Not falcon pills, nor pheasants fair,
Nor Dan's most artful trap—the hare—
Will catch Electors who don't care
For Johnny not a fig.

8.

Now Bill a sammywiller is—
Just look at his fine open phiz—
A jolly brick in hand he is,
And he will win the prize.

9.

Into the house right he will go,
And Johnny will cry, " Oh, dear, oh !"
My money in the stones don't show—
Oh ! what a great surprise !

Bill Carington he is the man,
Electors serve him all you can.

LEFT: Carrington acrostic; RIGHT: election
poems for Lord Carrington.

BEYOND THE BOUNDS

In Norman times, the hamlets along the river Wye were referred to as 'The Wicombes' and much more recently, in 1977, Jim Cottrell described the town as consisting of several Wycombes, comprising the town centre from Queens' Square to Crendon Street; the Easton Street area, almost like a village High Street; the St Mary Street and Lily's Walk area, full of picturesque cottages and fine houses; and the Newlands area, not so picturesque, but friendly and companionable. Much of this has gone, so it is interesting to retrace the town's growth between 1850 and 1900.

The population of Wycombe, according to the census of 1851 was 7,179, and ten years later, in 1861 it had grown to 8,375, an increase of 1,196; by the 1901 census the population had built up to 17,683. With such an increase there had been a corresponding expansion in the town itself, which made it necessary to extend the boundaries in 1880 and 1901, so, as to include the more recently laid out streets and roads. In 1851 the Borough extended from the bridge in St Mary Street (opposite the Anchor) in the south, to Bower Hayes (Castle Hill) in the north, and from Holywell Mead on the east (open-air swimming pool) to Wynkle's Bridge in the west. It was divided into four wards: Paul's Row, Frogmoor, High Street and Easton Wards. The opening of the railway station on Amersham Hill led, in the course of some years, to the formation of Castle Street, to provide a convenient and direct link between the Station and the West End of the town, so that the longer route round by the then narrow Crendon Lane could be avoided.

The town then began to spread out on each side. North Town arose on the sites of Wheeler's Field and Saffron Platt in one direction, while Denmark Street, Mendy Street, Temple Street, West End Road etc, were laid out in the other. Remington Terrace was named after Mr J. Remington Mills, who was elected Member of Parliament for the Borough in 1862, on the death of Sir G.H. Dashwood. The West End of the town developed rapidly; Oak Mead, as its name indicates, was an extensive piece of pasture land, and new streets sprang up there almost at once. Where Desborough Road now runs was a narrow way called Water-Lane which led towards West Wycombe, south of the River Wye, until Sir Francis Dashwood built the straight new road in the mid-18th century. The old Green Street was a portion of an ancient way, which ran from Desborough via Frogmoor, formerly called 'la Grene' and, passing the Green Farm off Hughenden Road, took its way up Green Hill to the old British encampment, and then according to R.S. Downs through Hazlemere, across the valley to the Watling Street.

The Desborough Field was laid out in streets with new roads running at right angles to the West Wycombe Road. On the other side, Kitchener Road, Oakbridge Road etc had been laid out.

On the south side of the town, little building took place but, on the north, the town extended itself considerably. The houses on the bank in the Hughenden Road were erected first and, some years later, residences were erected near the Hughenden

Brook; the Lower Temple Farm was converted into the Temple Chair Works, while opposite, the new County Police Station was erected in 1870. Later still, Benjamin Road, so called from the old name of the field in which it was laid out, and Roberts Road were formed. The Cemetery Road, later called Priory Road, was made up in 1855, and all the houses there were erected between 1855 and 1900. To form a connection between Cemetery Road and Amersham Hill and Totteridge Road, Priory Avenue was laid out and, during its construction, an Anglo-Saxon gold ornament was discovered. Priory Avenue, about 1900, was extended westward to join Hughenden Road.

In the central part of the town, some dilapidated timber and plaster houses were removed from the bottom of Crendon Street; Corporation Street was formed and, in Easton Street, improvements were made by the removal of a 15th century building known as 'Ebenezer' in 1887, which stood near the Grammar School and had been used as a meeting house by the Methodists until 1863. The new almshouses, built in Elizabethan Tudor style, were erected opposite the Grammar School on the site of the old Borough Workhouse, and most of the houses in London Road were erected in this period. The old Saw Mill and little beer-shop, known as 'The Rose', were removed, and a row of modern houses facing the Rye built.

Then came Gordon Road, which perpetuates the memory of the hero of Khartoum, and Conegra Road, which continues a name handed down from Celtic days. Spring Gardens as a location goes back at least to 1775, but was only built on in the 1890s. The last changes of the period were the formation of Queen Victoria Road, which connected the High Street with St Mary Street, and on its western side, the new Town Hall, opened in October 1904.

With the exception of the wide High Street, all the thoroughfares in other parts of the town were narrow and winding, hence they received the name 'The Narrows'. In early days there was little traffic but, as trade increased, there was a constant traffic of vans laden with heavy loads of chairs, and trucks carrying tons of timber, while the streets also began to be busy with tradesmen's carts, besides traps and carriages used for pleasure. Black spots began to be cleared, such as the widening of Church Street and Queen Square; also the bottom of Easton Street.

Both traffic and pedestrians were helped, but in 1850, with the exception of some favoured spots in the principal street, little had been accomplished in the way of paving. The pavements, where they existed, formed a kind of mosaic, composed of York Stone, Wycombe Stone, and here and there a patch of plain earth. About 1860 the main streets were paved with flagstones at the joint expense of the Corporation and Mr J.R. Mills, then Member of Parliament for the Borough. After this, other pavements were laid down with pebbly gravel and asphalt.

An important improvement to Frogmoor was made in 1877, when it was formally opened by J.O. Griffiths, covered with flagstones, kerbed and supplied with trees and a fountain. The Methodists built a new church in White Hart Street in 1875, and their old meeting house in Frogmoor was fitted up for public gatherings and renamed 'Frogmore Hall'. In May 1882, this was converted into Barracks for the Salvation Army.

In the middle of the nineteenth century, there were only two 'clubs' in the town, the Amicable and Literary Institution which was established in 1844 and the Mechanics Institute, founded a few years later. Both provided papers, magazines and periodicals for their members, occasionally arranged lectures on instructional topics, and had a small library. These became amalgamated in 1881 and moved to the little Market House as the Literary and Scientific Institute. The Conservative Club was founded in 1885, and started off in rooms in 28 High Street, then moved to 41 High Street, moving back to No 28, with a new building of which the foundation stone was laid in 1896, and the Club opened in December 1899. The Liberal Club was established in premises in the High Street which had been the former Mechanics Institute, and eventually moved to the present premises next to the Police Station, just round the corner from Queen Victoria Road. The Parish Church of All Saints was thoroughly restored inside in 1873-75, and outside in 1887-89. The high pews were cut down in 1865 and then replaced with chairs about 1875. The large pew belonging to the Marquis of Landsdowne was removed from the chancel arch in 1858 and eventually to Wycombe Abbey in 1891.

Chapel building was also popular, and the Wesleyans moved into the new Cemetery Road in 1875 with 'Priory Road Chapel', while the Primitive Methodists turned to Arthur Vernon for the designs of their new chapel in White Hart Street which was built in the same year. Also designed by Arthur Vernon was the church of the breakaway parish 'Christchurch' which was built in Crendon Lane between 1889 and 1897. This was demolished like the White Hart chapel in the mid-20th century in the name of progress; Priory Road survives as the centre of controversy over its future and proposed extensions.

This period also saw the demise of the Wycombe Fair, which took place on the Monday and Tuesday preceding the Feast of St Michael the Archangel which, up to 1871, was held within the Borough; then it became such a nuisance, that the townspeople petitioned for its suppresion. None of the caravans, shows, exhibitions, menageries etc, were allowed to come within the Borough boundaries until 9 o'clock on the Sunday evening before the opening of the Fair the following day. In consequence, they gathered outside the town and, directly the clock struck the hour, there was a wild rush into the streets to obtain favoured positions, the High Street of course being the most sought after. There would be an influx of visitors; there would be wild beast shows, ginger bread stalls, boxing booths, swings, donkey racing, dancing, and all the rest of the fun of the fair and, as the schools were not open during the week, everyone had a chance to enjoy it all.

On one occasion, three young lions escaped from their cage in the High Street; one of them unconcernedly lay down in the road in front of the shop occupied by Messrs Rolls Bros. On another occasion a bear managed to escape, to be rounded up from the fields at Saunderton the next evening. Although there were still many who wished to retain the fair, particularly in view of the fact that it was a 'Hiring Fair', the opposition, which was largely the townspeople living in the centre of High Wycombe, won the day, and the Fair was legally abolished by order of the Secretary of State in November 1871.

THE OLD COUNTRY

ABOVE: High Wycombe from the Oxford Road 1793; BELOW:
High Wycombe from Daws Hill c1930.

ABOVE AND BELOW: Views across High Wycombe c1900.

ABOVE AND BELOW: Views across High Wycombe c1900.

ABOVE: View across High Wycombe c1900; BELOW: Station
Yard looking into Castle Street c1910.

ABOVE: Amersham Hill c1910; BELOW: The Grange, Amersham
Hill 1907, built for Walter Birch.

45

ABOVE: Amersham Hill at Terriers 1909; CENTRE LEFT: Toll House at Terriers c1930;
CENTRE RIGHT: Water Tower, Tower Street, 1911; BELOW: Terriers c1920.

46

ABOVE: Top of Totteridge Lane c1910; LEFT: Hatters Lane 1911; RIGHT: Lane leading from Keep Hill to Marsh Green c1890.

47

ABOVE: Town Hall seen from pond at Marsh Green; BELOW:
Bowerdean Farm c1900.

ABOVE: Hicks Farm c1900; BELOW: Hicks Farmlands c1930.

ABOVE: Haywards Cottage on River Wye c1920; BELOW:
Bassetsbury Manor 1925 before restoration.

ABOVE: Smith's Farm, Booker c1890; BELOW: Loakes House.

ABOVE: The Dyke c1910; CENTRE: Downley Common c1920;
BELOW: Desborough House, built for J. Parker.

52

ALL THE FUN OF THE FAIR

It is traditionally believed that most people made their own entertainment in the past, and bored later generations are frequently reminded of that fact. Into most villages and towns would come the itinerant players and entertainers at fair-time, or on festivals, which were often well attended. In addition to the normal markets from which Chepping Wycombe gets its name, both the Hospital of St Giles, which was a Leper Hospital on the outskirts of the mediaeval borough, and also the Hospital of St John had fairs. These were by grants from the Royal court, for Henry III approved a fair, to take place on the Eve and Feast of the Translation of St Thomas a Becket (7 July) to St John's, and the Leper Hospital was granted a fair of two days on the Eve and Feast of St Margaret (20 July).

The proximity of Windsor might be the reason for the presence in Wycombe of a group of actors in Tudor times, for the Royal Household Accounts for 1492-1509 mentioned several companies of players, including one attached to the town of Wycombe. A Royal musician was also connected with the town, as the Parish Church was the final resting place of Ferdinando Norton 'one of His Majesty's Band of Musicians', who died in 1779. Drama was also represented in the later eighteenth century by a Playhouse or Theatre in St Mary Street, which was probably largely frequented by the military officers and their wives from the Military Academy in High Street. Earlier there had been a bowling alley in the 17th century, whose attendant was John Sharpe. He was formally called the Keeper of the Bowling Green, and the site would most likely have been at the Crendon Road end of Castle Street, as records show that the property of Thomas Oliffe, known as 'The White House', in High Street, ran northwards to 'a place there called the Lower Bowling Alley'. The Rye was also a place of entertainment, and by ancient tradition certain 'Law Days' were held on the Rye, when the Burgesses and others gathered together for bye-laws to be passed and other annual business of the Corporation was transacted. These were extended into more social events, for in the 18th century 'All the inhabitants of the Borough have liberty at all times to walk, and use sports and pastimes such as running, leaping, wrestling, riding, backswords and other plays at their pleasure, without being trespassers, the liberty of using these exercises is much valued by the Common people'.

Entertainment on the Rye could sometimes have a more macabre element as on the occasion in 1736, when two murderers, Marsh and Marshall, were hung following the death of Mr Pontifax, a farmer returning home to Downley from Wycombe Market. The crowd that arrived to see the event was so dense that part of the Grammar School wall was knocked down. Booths and stalls were erected, and the gibbet was built 28 feet high to ensure that all could see the spectacle. It was Dr Johnson who rather trenchantly commented 'Executions are intended to draw spectators, if they do not draw spectators, they don't answer their purpose'. In order to press home the point, the remains of the executed men were left hanging in chains for several years, until removed at the wish of the occupants of Wycombe Abbey. A

few years later, when another hanging was announced, the stalls and booths went up again but, when the news filtered through that the man had been hanged at Aylesbury to avoid expected trouble, the crowd came near to rioting, robbed as they were of their entertainment. The rights on the Rye were not always honoured in the way that earlier comment suggests, for in 1882 a byelaw was passed because of the increasing instances of naked bathing in the Dyke, and earlier, in 1870, the magistrates were amazed to hear that it had been necessary for the police to chase some cricketers off the Rye, for playing there on a Sunday.

The Rye had been a traditional place for cricket matches for some time, with the earliest recorded being a match played in July 1774:

'*Cricket Match.* To be played for on Wycombe Rye, in the County of Bucks, between the Gentlemen of the above County and the Gentlemen of Risborough Club, on Wednesday the 27th instant. A SILVER CUP, value Five Guineas, given gratis by a few Innkeepers of Wycombe; and a considerable sum of money is likewise depending, it being the third match played between the two parties. The wickets to be pitched precisely at Ten O'clock in the forenoon, and the match to be played out.

N.B. There will be Twelve Hats given gratis to be played for at Backswords, on Saturday the 30th instant, at Wycombe aforesaid, by twelve men on a side; and every man that breaks a head is entitled to a Hat, and the Umpire of that Side which breaks the most Heads, is likewise entitled to a Hat.'

The actual site of the cricket ground in th 19th century is shown on the transcript of a lease of November 1838 to John Neale from Lord Carrington, and it was known as Dryclose field. It was described as containing 4 acres, 1 rood and 19 perches, with 314 feet frontage on London Road, and 310 feet on Bassetsbury Lane and extending south to the River Wye. Another 'Grand Match between the Clubs of Aylesbury and High Wycombe' was reported in the *Bucks, Berks and Herts Chronicle* of August 1827, which seemed to go on all day for, although it started at 9 o'clock in the morning, the report reads that 'soon after sunset they (Wycombe) had made 95 runs, and had only five men put out. William Marshall, who appeared much distressed complained that he could not see the ball and wished to leave off for the night. The Aylesbury men objected to this . . . and they recommended play' and Wycombe men kept their wickets up till they got 32 runs more, which gave them the game. The following week a return match was announced under the heading 'When Greek meets Greek' and this took place on the Rye, with Wycombe winning once again, after which 'both parties resorted to the Swan Inn, and partook of an excellent dinner, and spent the evening with the utmost hilarity and good humour'.

Besides the attractions of the Rye itself, the River Wye 'was for centuries deservedly celebrated as one of the purest and best of the small streams in England, not only for sport with the fly-rod, but for the edible qualities of the trout it so freely produced, for their perfect form, beautiful marking, and sheen of silver shading to gold'. Nowadays we automatically refer to the river as 'The Wye', but in 1912 the writer of this article had to explain that 'the Wick as it is always locally called throughout its whole course of ten and a half miles from where it rises near West

Wycombe to its outfall in the Thames; is often written and in books referred to as the Wye'. In the past it was known as the Wycombe Stream, as Newland Brook, or simply as 'the river'. Writing in 1848, Kingsley quotes a source as finding 'In some parts of the stream trout are very numerous, and of course not very large, the average being about three-quarters of a pound weight, but I have taken fish there upwards of three pounds. At Mr Street's mill (Mr Saunder's Wycombe Marsh), a little below Wycombe, where the water is well preserved, I once killed twenty brace of fine trout in four hours'. The catches of one angler between 1881 and 1889 were recorded as between 36 and 64 brace in a year, but by 1901 it was reported that 'the fishing here is a thing of the past, I think in a year or two the famous Wycombe trout will have become extinct', and the High Wycombe Angling and Trout Preservation Association was wound up in February 1901.

Societies may come and go, but certain aspects of life go on forever. When the Wycombe Horticultural Society died in 1857, the *Bucks Free Press* regretted that 'The beerhouse is not the choice but the necessity of the working man' while in the same paper two years later is the report of a wife who complained of the bad example set when her twelve-year old son came home tottering, having drunk a good part of his wages. We tend to forget the importance of beer to the working man in the mid-19th century. In 1872 the Magistrates were approached to extend the start of licensing hours to 5.00 am in the summer and 6.00 am in the winter, as 'the men call on their way to work in the fields at five o'clock, and in many cases the beerhouse keepers were in the habit of sending out beer to the fields at that hour.'

The size of the problem is apparent when reading the long list of public houses and beerhouses in High Wycombe, which is woven into a tale published in the *Bucks Free Press*, in 1928 — 'Innsigns of the Times — a trip round Wycombe:
"The Queen" wearing "The Rose and Crown" and "The Golden Fleece" accompanied by "King George V" and "Victoria", escorted by "The Iron Duke" and "The Red Cross Knight", went on a voyage in "The Ship" round "The Globe" as far as "Bell Vue". After a "Roundabout" cruise they cast "Anchor" near the "Royal Oak" in time to see "The Falcon" and "The Swan" fly into the "Arms of Beaconsfield". They also saw "The Jolly Butcher" drive "The White Horse" in "The Van" with the "Two Brewers" and "Three Tuns". They called at "The Carrington Arms", sat on "The Woolpack" and enjoyed a snack of "Pheasant" and "Pineapple"; a "Bird in Hand" is worth two in the bush. After reading "The Morning Star" by the light of "The Half Moon" they saw "The Fox" looking at "The Nags Head" on "The Gate" of "The Flint Cottage". He suddenly rang "The Bell" which caused "The Bull" and "The Red Cow" to bolt through the town as far as "The Railway Tavern" where they collided with "The Horse and Jockey", broke "The Porters Arms" and cracked "The Saracens Head". "The Black Boy" shouted out be careful old "Cock" Keep within "the Compass" or "The Mason's Arms" will soon grab you. Suddenly "The Rifle Butts" in and wanted to know what made his "A(u)ntelope" she always looked like an "Angel" especially when in "The Chairmakers' Arms" and he would not "Exchange" her for a "White Blackbird" or a "Mother Redcap" but would sooner "Plough" the land with a "Steam Engine".

Here, hear, quoth "The Red Lion", "The White Hart" and "The Black Swan". At that moment "The Cow and Hare" tried to sing a duet, but they sang in such "Cross Keys" that "The White Lion" said they were making a "Hard" job of it and should be "Ledbetter". Harmony reigned once more and everybody was proud as a "Peacock" when they saw "The King's Head" nodding to them as they drove by in "The Coach and Horses". They all "Rose" and saluted. "Gordon Arms" then called the landlord and said fill "(H)our Glass" at "The Fountain" there is a "Friend at Hand" so we'll pop round to the "Desborough" where there will be a "Happy Union" under the shade of the old "Beech Tree".'

The obvious answer to such an onslaught of licensed houses was religion, and the chapels in the 19th century played an active part in the life of the community. They had their Bible readings or study classes as well as their tennis clubs and cycling groups; they had their choral excesses as well as quite successful football teams, but above all, they had their Sunday Schools, which followed in the tradition of Hannah Ball. Of all the events of the Sunday School calendar, the Sunday School Treat stood out as a red-letter day; children had even been known to change from one Sunday School to another, in order to benefit from these outings. They varied from that of the Chapel in Crendon Lane when three hundred children went by rail to Marlow and then by barge along the Thames, to the strains of the Wycombe Brass Band, to the more regimented children of the Newland Baptist Chapel, who marched in line to Kings Wood at Totteridge, marching back probably rather tired and sticky.

Even more spectacular were the great treats of the great Old Queen's Jubilees. On the occasion of Her Majesty's Diamond Celebrations in June 1897, the children assembled at 2.30 in different parts of the town and then marched 'their various routes to the High Street under the care of Superintendents and teachers, and great credit is due to those in authority for the order and nicety in which the massing of some 4,600 children and their progress into the Park, (Wycombe Abbey Grounds), was accomplished. When all the schools were in position, a bugle was the signal for the singing of the doxology and a verse of the National Anthem. It must be admitted that the choral effect was not so effective as the scenic display! It was just before four o'clock that the signal was given for the singing of grace; then the youngsters fell with vigour on the excellent provisions set before them. Great urns of tea were quickly emptied, plates of bread and butter and cakes were cleared with magical rapidity, and the feast was evidently enjoyed by one and all of the guests'.

But even such innocent connections as Sunday Schools had their pitfalls for, in a letter of 1858 in the *Bucks Free Press,* a Sunday School leader asked 'can the teachers who assiduously and laboriously endeavour every Sunday to wean the minds of the children . . . from the vanity of things below, see them, without one pang of regret, being initiated in all kinds of worldly amusements and their love of pomp and show fostered and encouraged by being plunged into all the excitement of what is called a Sunday School Treat'.

The writer of this letter would have been appalled to know of the receipt made out to J. Pepalle, dated 27 July 1853, for 7 gallons of beer purchased by the Wesleyan Sunday School at a cost of 16 pence per gallon.

The night life of High Wycombe, while not riotous, offered various enjoyments to the local man and woman about town. A Public Concert for 2 January 1828 was held in the Town Hall (now the Guildhall) and it offered works by Handel, Haydn, Guglielmi, Callcot, Webbe, Bishop and others, with admission 'Ladies and Gentlemen 5s; Juvenile branches of the family 3s.6d each'. These high prices may well have kept the numbers down; not so in the case of a choral rendition of Handel's *Messiah* in 1857, when an entrance fee of twopence ensured an audience of 500 people (plus choir and musicians) in a hall capable of holding 350 persons, so they must have been crammed in like sardines.

Uplifting events took place such as a lecture on the late Earl of Beaconsfield by Henry W. Taunt, illustrated by OXY-HYDROGEN LANTERN which vied for popularity with such low-class humour as Monsieur Boaz, the conjuror, who used to eat knives and forks, and astonish the spectators by frying pancakes and eggs in his hat. To add to the entertainment facilities of the town, the Central Hall in High Street was re-fitted, enlarged and newly arranged by Mr R.D. Vernon, to be suitable for theatrical performances, and was soon patronised by companies on provincial tours, local societies for concerts and similar entertainments. Unfortunately the hall only lasted until about 1899, as it was on the site of the present Corporation Street, and so it was demolished to allow the link road from High Street to Castle Street in 1900.

The present Town Hall followed shortly afterwards in 1904 in the new 'Queen Victoria Road', which lay roughly on the line of the former carriageway to Wycombe Abbey from High Street. The organ was installed in 1905, purchased from St James Hall, Piccadilly. The Red Room (now the Oak Room) was embellished with five stained windows designed by Arthur J. Dix and presented by the Raffety Family in 1911.

It was not long before the silver screen made its appearance in the town, with the 'Palace' opening in Frogmoor in 1909 on a site opposite its present position. The 'Electric Theatre' came a little later in Oxford Street and was also in Frogmoor. Other cinemas included 'The Rex' (1912), 'The Grand' (1913) and 'The Majestic' (1930) later renamed 'The Odeon'. The opening of the Handy Cross Sports Centre in the 1970s reminds us of the many outdoor and indoor sports and swimming clubs and associations which have thrived, declined and been re-vitalised from time to time in the area, and it seems fitting at the moment, when the marathon and half-marathon are the current forms of extreme exertion, to find in the newspaper files that in June 1903 the solicitors' clerks of High Wycombe organised a walk from High Wycombe to Marble Arch (twenty-nine miles). The route was from Wycombe Town Hall via Wycombe Marsh, Beaconsfield, Gerrards Cross, Uxbridge, Southall, Hanwell, Acton, Ealing, Shepherds Bush, Notting Hill and Bayswater. There were to be no walking or pacing sticks, and the competitors had to carry their own refreshments or purchase them on the road. There were sixteen starters and twelve finished, the winner being H.R. Vickers (from Mr J. Bliss's office) who finished the course in 6 hrs 12 mins 30 secs, an average of 4.67 miles per hour. Vickers received a handsome chair and a silver medal with a gold centre . . . last man home received a wooden spoon.

HIGH SOCIETY

ABOVE: Wedding group, Castle Hill House 1901; CENTRE: Cricket Ground, London Road, 1901; BELOW: Fryer Mill Bathing Pool 1928.

ABOVE: Aleck Stacey's Swimming Pool, Frogmore 1910;
BELOW: Sunday School outing to Daws Hill Park c1900.

HIGH WYCOMBE.

OPENING OF THE
COTTAGE HOSPITAL.

THE RIGHT HON. LORD CARINGTON

Having kindly consented to conduct the formal opening of the Hospital, the Committee respectfully invite their Friends to meet his Lordship on the Ground at 12 o'clock a.m.

ON TUESDAY, AUGUST 24th, 1875,

Immediately after which they will adjourn to the grounds of Castle Hill, where, by kind permission of JOHN EDWARDS, Esq., a large Marquee will be erected for the purpose of holding a

FANCY BAZAAR,

WHICH WILL BE OPENED TWO DAYS, FOR THE

Sale of Articles of Needlework, Ornaments, &c.

LADY PATRONESSES:

THE RIGHT HON. LADY CARINGTON,
HER GRACE THE DUCHESS OF WESTMINSTER,
THE RIGHT HON. LADY BOSTON,
THE HON. MRS. CARINGTON,
LADY ROSE,
THE HON. MRS. HALL,
LADY HARVEY,

THE HON. MRS. PRATT, Oving,
MRS. T. O. WETHERED,
MRS. GILBEY, Wooburn House,
MRS. ELLAMES, Little Marlow,
MRS. CHILTON, Vicarage, High Wycombe,
MRS. HEWETT, Uplands House,

LADIES' COMMITTEE:

MRS. PARKER,
„ TUCK,
„ J. PARKER,
„ MARSHALL,

MRS. B. LUCAS,
„ H. TURNER,
„ D. CLARKE,
„ THURLOW,
MRS. F. WHEELER, Secretary.

MRS. DAVIES,
„ DUNSTAN,
„ R. VERNON,
MISS E. WHEELER.

STALL HOLDERS:

1. MRS. GROOME, MRS. J. PARKER, MRS. H. TURNER.
2. MRS. AND THE MISSES PARKER, AND THE MISSES VERNON.
3. MRS. B. LUCAS AND MRS. ETHERINGTON.
4. MRS. F. BENHAM.
5. MRS. DAVIES, MRS. DUNSTAN, MISS DREWETT.
6. MRS. RUCKLEY AND THE MISSES PEPIN.
7. MRS. F. WHEELER, MISS ESTHER WHEELER, MISS B. WHEELER.
8. Flowers, Ferns, &c.—MRS. F. WHEELER AND MISS ROBINSON.
9. MRS. C. SKULL & MISS SKULL—Chair Stall.
10. Refreshment Stall: MRS. AND THE MISSES GILES, MRS. AND THE MISSES GILBERT.

THE BAZAAR WILL OPEN AT 1 O'CLOCK ON TUESDAY, AND AT ½ O'CLOCK ON WEDNESDAY,

CLOSING EACH DAY AT NINE O'CLOCK.

Admission on the first day, 1s.; the second day, 6d.; after Six o'clock, the first day, half-price. Children half-price each day. Ticket holders may inspect the Hospital building.

Contributions of Useful and Fancy Articles will be thankfully received by any Member of the Ladies' Committee or any of the Stall-holders, on or before Saturday, August 20th. Ferns, Flowers, and Fruit, on the mornings of the Bazaar.

A REFRESHMENT STALL WILL BE PROVIDED.

Tickets to be obtained of Mr. Judson, Mr. F. J. Westfield, Mr. F. Young, and at the Gate.

Cottage Hospital — programme of opening 1873.

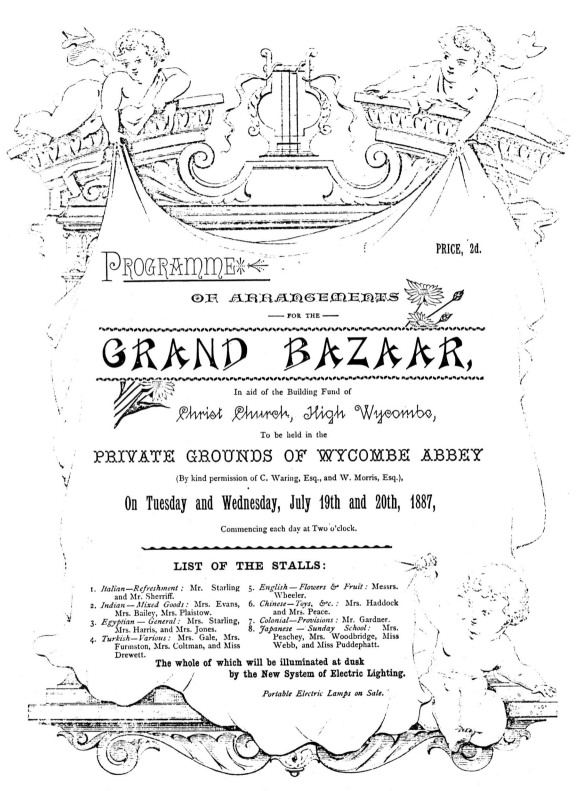

PRICE, 2d.

PROGRAMME

OF ARRANGEMENTS

— FOR THE —

GRAND BAZAAR,

In aid of the Building Fund of

Christ Church, High Wycombe,

To be held in the

PRIVATE GROUNDS OF WYCOMBE ABBEY

(By kind permission of C. Waring, Esq., and W. Morris, Esq.),

On Tuesday and Wednesday, July 19th and 20th, 1887,

Commencing each day at Two o'clock.

LIST OF THE STALLS:

1. *Italian—Refreshment :* Mr. Starling and Mr. Sherriff.
2. *Indian — Mixed Goods :* Mrs. Evans, Mrs. Bailey, Mrs. Plaistow.
3. *Egyptian — General :* Mrs. Starling, Mrs. Harris, and Mrs. Jones.
4. *Turkish—Various :* Mrs. Gale, Mrs. Furmston, Mrs. Coltman, and Miss Drewett.
5. *English — Flowers & Fruit :* Messrs. Wheeler.
6. *Chinese—Toys, &c. :* Mrs. Haddock and Mrs. Peace.
7. *Colonial—Provisions :* Mr. Gardner.
8. *Japanese — Sunday School :* Mrs. Peachey, Mrs. Woodbridge, Miss Webb, and Miss Puddephatt.

The whole of which will be illuminated at dusk by the New System of Electric Lighting.

Portable Electric Lamps on Sale.

Wycombe Abbey — Grand Bazaar 1887.

BOROUGH OF CHEPPING WYCOMBE.

NEW TOWN HALL.

Programme.—Opening Ceremony,

WEDNESDAY, OCTOBER 12th, 1904.

THE TOWN COUNCIL to assemble in their Robes of Office at the Council Chamber at 12 45, and accompany the Mayor to the New Town Hall.

THE REV. E. D. SHAW, Vicar of the Parish, to offer Prayer at the Entrance to the Hall.

THE MAYOR to formally Open the Building.

PUBLIC LUNCHEON IN THE HALL.

Toasts.

To Propose		To Respond
THE MAYOR	"The King."	
	National Anthem.	
THE MAYOR ...	"The Queen, Prince and Princess of Wales, and rest of the Royal Family."	
EARL CARRINGTON ...	"Success to New Hall." ..	{ THE RECORDER, E. J. PAYNE, ESQ., MA.
Song ... "I know a lovely Garden," by Guy d'Hardlot ... Miss Florence Wane.		
THE MAYOR	{ "Our Neighbouring Municipalities, and District Councils."	{ THE MAYOR, MAIDENHEAD THE MAYOR, HENLEY-ON-THAMES. MR. J. STRATFOLD READ, J.P.
ALDERMAN PEACE, J.P. ...	"Our Visitors." ...	{ SIR R. J. DASHWOOD, BART. T. A. HERBERT, ESQ.
Song ... ... "Vanity Fair," by G. H. Clutsam ... Miss Florence Wane.		
ALDERMAN VERNON, J.P.	"The Architects and Builders." .	{ MR. BATEMAN. MR. C. H. HUNT.
Song ... "My Garden of Roses," by Florence Aylward... Miss Florence Wane.		
MR. F. M. BRIDGEWATER	{ "The Town and Trade of Wycombe."	{ ALDERMAN BIRCH, J.P. ALDERMAN DEACON, J.P.

Opening of new Town Hall — programme 1904.

RUSTIC FANCY FAIR
AND
SUMMER FÊTE,
IN
LORD CARRINGTON'S PARK,
(In aid of the Wycombe Free Library Endowment Fund),
JULY 18, 19, & 20, 1882.

RUSTIC ARBOUR STALLS,

Flower and Fruit Stall.
Artisan's Stall, &c.,
Handsomely decorated. To be
Opened by Lady Carrington at Two o'clock on Tuesday.
Military Band each day.
Lawn Tennis, Cricket, and Archery.
Concert in the Abbey.
Ventriloquial Entertainment by Professor Le Marc.
Art Loan Exhibition.
Handbell Ringers.
Drum and Fife Band, &c , &c.
Breaks will run from the Park at intervals to Hughenden Manor
To allow Visitors to see the Ancient Church,
The Queen's Memorial, &c.

REFRESHMENT TENT ON THE GROUNDS.

Admission to the Fair :—
First Day, 2/6. After 6 o'clock, 1/-. Second Day
(Wednesday) 1/-. Third day 6d. Children under Twelve
Half-price.

If bought by Saturday previous, as under :—
First day, Single, 2/-. To admit Three, 5/-., or Season
Single Tickets, 3/-, of Mr. Westfield, Messrs. Butler
Bros., High Wycombe, or from

WYCOMBE ABBEY
RUSTIC FANCY FAIR.

SPECIAL ATTRACTION.

The Committee have been successful in arranging
with the Provincial Brush Electric Light Company
to supply

THE ELECTRIC LIGHT

To illuminate the Stalls each evening.

*This will be the first Public Exhibition of the
Electric Light in the County of Bucks.*

Entrance to the Park Grounds will be either by the
" Rupert Gate " in the High Street, or the Lodge
Gates in St. Mary Street, and on Keep Hill.

NO PERSON WILL BE ADMITTED WITHOUT A TICKET.

Wycombe Abbey — Rustic Fancy Fair 1882.

GREAT WESTERN RAILWAY.

RUSTIC FANCY FAIR
AND
SUMMER FÊTE
IN
WYCOMBE ABBEY PARK,
JULY 18, 19, & 20, 1882.

RETURN TICKETS TO HIGH WYCOMBE

Will be issued from Stations named below, on and after Monday, July 17th,
available by all Trains up to the following Monday, July 24th inclusive,
at the following greatly reduced rates.

STATIONS.	3rd. s. d.	2nd. s. d.	1st. s. d.
Paddington	3 11	6 0	8 2
Acton	3 5	5 2	7 1
Ealing	3 2	4 11	6 11
Castle Hill	3 2	4 11	6 11
Hanwell	3 0	4 10	6 8
Southall	2 11	4 6	6 3
Brentford	3 2	4 11	6 11
Hayes	2 8	4 2	6 0
West Drayton	2 5	3 9	5 4
Uxbridge	2 8	4 0	5 8
Langley	2 1	3 4	4 9
Slough	1 10	3 1	4 5
Windsor	2 1	3 6	4 11
Taplow	1 5	2 5	3 7
Maidenhead	1 1	2 1	3 2
Twyford	2 1	3 8	5 2
Henley	2 6	4 2	6 0
Reading	2 6	4 6	6 3
Cookham	0 9	1 6	2 3
Bourne End	0 8	1 3	2 1
Great Marlow	1 1	1 11	2 10
Wooburn Green	0 7	0 10	1 3
Loudwater	0 4	0 8	1 0
West Wycombe	0 4	0 5	0 8
Princes Risboro'	1 0	1 8	2 6
Little Kimble	1 3	2 3	3 4
Aylesbury	1 10	3 2	4 9
Bledlow	1 1	2 1	3 2
Thame	1 6	2 11	4 5
Teddington	2 1	3 5	5 8
Wheatley	2 4	4 5	6 6
Littlemore	2 9	5 4	7 5

HIGH WYCOMBE FANCY FAIR
AND
SUMMER FÊTE,
IN AID OF THE FREE LIBRARY ENDOWMENT FUND.

JULY 18, 19, & 20, 1882.

On Tuesday, the first day of the RUSTIC FANCY FAIR
at Wycombe Abbey, Two

GRAND CONCERTS

Will be given in the DINING ROOM of the ABBEY, by
kind permission and under the superintendence of

LADY CARRINGTON.

The following distinguished Lady and Gentlemen Amateurs and Artistes
have kindly consented to assist :—

The VISCOUNTESS FOLKESTONE.
The VISCOUNTESS DOWNE.
The HONBLE. MRS. E. BOURKE.
LORD WILLIAM COMPTON.
SIGNOR F. PAOLO TOSTI.
MR. WILLIAM H. LESLIE (VIOLIN).

The undermentioned Ladies will form the chorus, under the direction of
SIGNOR F. P. TOSTI :—

The Marchioness of Waterford	The Lady Feodore Yorke
The Countess Cowper	The Lady Carrington
The Countess of Romney	The Honble. Mrs. Dawnay
The Countess of Clarendon	The Honble. Mrs. E. Bourke
The Countess of Antrim	The Honble. Alice Harbord
The Viscountess Downe	Miss Mary Liddell
The Viscountess Folkestone	Miss Somers Cocks
The Lady Margaret Compton	AND
The Lady Florence Duncombe	Miss Grey

The First Concert will commence at 4 o'clock, Tickets for Front Rows, 10s. :
Second Rows, 5s. The Second Concert will commence at 6.15 p.m.; Tickets
for the Front Rows, 5s. ; Second Rows, 2s. 6d.
Tickets may be obtained, in advance, of Mr. F. Westfield, and of Messrs.
Butler Bros , High Wycombe : or from the Stall-Holders at the Fair.
For a List of the General Attractions of the Fancy Fair see other side.

C. W. RAFFETY, } Honorary
C. T. BAINES. } Secretaries.

FRONT OF THEATRE

PROSCENIUM

Souvenir programme of opening of Majestic Theatre 1930.

ABOVE: 'Bannermans Cup' factory race 1912/13; BELOW:
Loakes Park, opening of Tennis Club 1903.

ABOVE: High Wycombe Trinity Football Club 1912/13; BELOW:
High Wycombe Cricket Team 1883.

IN OTHER WORDS

It has been observed, not without a certain amount of truth, that High Wycombe can be considered a literary desert. While this candid view may seem hard, it is not apparently a new idea, for over a century ago, in 1862, Rachel Moorcock, whose family lived in this town, recorded an 'In Memoriam' following a disastrous lecture in the Town:

'Died, at High Wycombe, on the evening of the 14th of January 1862, *Literary Taste!*; It had been rapidly declining for some time. Its decease was announced by a medical gentleman, in the Town Hall, at twenty minutes past eight o'clock, and so deep was the sympathy manifested by the inhabitants of the town, that a popular and talented lecturer, who had been engaged by the Literary Institute to lecture on "Lord Byron", found himself confronted by empty benches instead of audience, and consequently retired without delivering the lecture. The mourning was much deeper than that worn for the late lamented Prince Consort, for at an entertainment given in the Town Hall on the following evening, the whole of the performers appeared with their skins blacked.'

> 'Oh Oratory! where is the magic spell,
> That once was thine? and souls would thrill
> And kindle into rapture at thy voice.
> Inspire my song, Milton, thou didst sing
> In lofty strains the loss of paradise,
> Cowper, I would invoke thy presence too,
> With all thy love of sentiment sublime,
> Thy scion of all that is noble, come
> And mourn our want of literary taste.
> Breathe on us now, and bid our spirits glow
> With nobler feeling, let pure taste revive.
> How shall foolish fancies take the place of rational delights,
>   and oratory
> Go begging for an audience.'

Rachel's comments, and her rather Victorian poetic flight of epic verse did not stop others, before and after, from describing our town in their own particular way. Henry Kingston in 1848 wrote an enjoyable but rambling history of the Borough in his *The History of Wycombe, with recollection of my native town* in which he includes his partisan view of what was then a small manufacturing country market town.

'The beech-clad hills of Bucks, which spontaneously adorn and beautify the Hundreds of Desborough, encompass not a more picturesque valley than it does the place where stands my native town. Sequested little spot! Adorned by nature with many delightful varieties of hill and dale, it seems to afford security for retirement; and those who love to watch the sparkling brook, and gaze with delight on the verdure and fertility of the surrounding pasture, in preference to luxury; or repose in the shade of the secluded woods, rather than seek the honours of princes, or the equinoctial

hurricanes of political notoriety, may dwell for a time in Wycombe, and "babble o' green fields".'

The lure of the River Wye, and the way in which it busily forced its way through the mills and pastures of the valley as it made its way down to the Thames, was also the subject of a longer poem by William Lane who in 1798 published his *Vale of Wycombe*:

'Delightful Valley! whose luxurious meads,
Crown'd with rich herbage floating to the breeze,
Enamell'd with the softest gayest blooms,
By nature's lib'ral land profusely spread;
And on each side the graceful hills arise,
Whose crops abundant clothe the fertile soil,
And promise to the peasant rich reward,
Striving to vie with the prolific vale.
Nor less the sylvan scenes their charms display,
Whose widespread foliage forms the cooling shade,
And sooths the languors of the fervid noon.
While down below Wick's fair, meand'ring stream,
Betwixt the bending willows steals along;
But soon arrested in her calm career,
Th' obstructing dam demands a transient pause;
She's then conducted to the torturing wheel,
Whose horrid crash thro' all the valley sounds!
Then quits with rapid flight the tyrant's paw;
But when to safer distances far arriv'd,
Her agitated breast becomes compos'd,
And as she roves along the sandy bed,
Her injuries in softest murmurs tells.'

Travellers also moved along the valley by road and their observations could be somewhat pointed. William Cobbett collected his *Rural Rides* in 1830 and recalled 'Passing through High Wycombe' including his somewhat scathing feelings about the major landowner of Wycombe Abbey, known locally as 'The Monk of Wycombe':

'When I got to High Wycombe, I found everything a week earlier than in the rich part of Hertfordshire. High Wycombe, as if the name was ironical, lies along the bottom of a narrow and deep valley, the hills on each side being very steep indeed. The valley runs somewhere about east to west, and the wheat on the hills facing the south will, if this weather continues, be fit to reap in ten days. I saw one field of oats that a bold farmer would cut next Monday. Wycombe is a very fine and very clean market town; the people all looking extremely well; the girls somewhat larger featured and larger boned than those in Sussex, and not as fresh-coloured and bright-eyed. More like the girls in America, and that is saying quite as much as any reasonable woman can expect or wish for.

The hills on the south side of Wycombe form a park and estate now the property of Smith, who was a banker or stock-maker at Nottingham, who was made a lord in the time of Pitt, and who purchased this estate of the late Marquis of Landsdowne, one of whose titles is Baron Wycombe. Wycombe is one of those famous things called boroughs, and 34 votes in this borough send Sir John Dashwood and Sir Thomas Baring to the 'collective wisdom' (i.e. Parliament). The landlord where I put up "remembered" the name of Dashwood but had "forgotten" who the other was! There would be no forgetting of this sort, if these thirty-four, together with their representatives, were called upon to pay the share of the national debt due from High Wycombe.'

But no less intolerant was the Corporation itself in the 18th century, whose stand for protestantism is apparent in the wording of the Oath sworn by the Bailiffs and other officials taking office with the Chepping Wycombe Corporation in 1752.

'I do swear that I do from my heart abhor, detest and abjure as Impious and heretical that Damnable doctrine and position that Princes Excommunicated or deprived by the Pope or any Authority or the See of Rome may be deposed or murdered by their subject or anyone whatsoever And I do declare that no foreign Prince, person, prelate, State or potentate, hath or ought to have any jurisdiction Power, Superiority, Preeminence, Authority, Ecclesiastical or Spiritual within this realme.

So help me God.'

Luckily a lighter element, as always, existed among the younger people of the town for, when Miss Sussannah Taylor married William West Medwin in 1802, he possibly won her hand with his loving acrostic based on the letters of her name. William Medwin had a malt house, granary and dwelling house in Frogmore, and his memoir and poems were published in 1882.

'ACROSTIC TO MISS TAYLOR
S-weetly she smiles, and with grace,
U-nsullied's the name of my dear
S-weet beauties I view in her face,
A-nd sweet is her voice in my ear.
N-or of cruelty can I complain,
N-ot a frown did she ever deserve,
A-nd from me she shall never have blame,
H-aving no fault but that of reserve.

T-hen away with reserve, love to say,
A-nd grant me the boon that I sue,
Y-ou must yield, you're content with the day,
L-et me name it for me to have you.
O-r, let me change my style, throw off your fetters,
R-eason and love to wed in these first letters.'

The town, its politics and Corporation were the continual butt for poems, cartoons and jokes published in the *Bucks Free Press,* or printed privately and sold, or circulated privately among the townspeople. Benjamin Disraeli and Lord Carrington

were two more popular subjects for these outbursts, but a more balanced view comes from the pen of F.W. Raffety with verses from his *Wycombe, our Town* written in 1944.

'Long years before we knew this place,
The early fathers of our race,
Though limited in thought and space,
Here lived and served their lot.
And though their outlook then was small,
No world unseen was practical,
A tiny town their all in all,
This was their much-loved spot.

They lived untouched by foreign wars,
The rival Roses left few scars,
When Red and White, by constant jars,
The feudal lords dethrone.
While others fight they pay their scot,
Father and son pursue their lot,
Thus slowly independence got,
To live upon their own

Wars of religion came more near,
And suffering brought too oft, I fear,
Before the Word was read out clear,
In Wycombe's ancient Church.
But Commonwealth had come too soon,
Though Restoration proved no boon,
The "Glorious Revolution"
Was Liberty's keystone.

So set amidst these famous shrines,
Midst names that history proud entwines,
Wycombe could not in its confines,
be "mute, inglorious".
Milton, and Cowper, Gray and Penn,
Seemed living still in living men,
What had been done to do again,
Their cause victorious.

Reform! and "Nothing but the Bill",
Held back by fear and force until,
The all prevailing people's will,
Its strength at last declares.
But change is but an idle dream,
In Wycombe much the same, I deem,
Quiet flowing in the Age of Steam,
Paper long before chairs.

Amazing son of Bradenham's squire,
Did ever son astonish sire!
Thrice to Parliament did aspire,
And thrice he was refused.
That was the choice of Wycombe's men,
Our grandmothers had no votes then,
To turn the scales for wondrous Ben,
They were the first bemused.

Cottagers, bodgers, chairmakers good,
Those early craftsmen in beechwood,
Long before chair factories stood,
And thousands worked indoors.
The contributions slowly flowed,
The horse vans stacked to highest load,
Starting at night by London Road,
Endless tiers of "Windsors".

The roads and inns then passed their prime,
The hour was yet far off to chime,
When cycles, motors, in their time,
Aid the situation.
The "Wycombe Branch" for long remains,
Great Western's hope of local gains,
Whoever dreamed that mainline trains,
Would pass by Wycombe Station!

And now the old Town disappears,
Changes prodigious mark the years,
Beyond our grandsires' utmost fears.
New roads, houses creeping all,
Along the valley up the hill,
Bright-lighted shops from gay street fill,
Van Winkle would stand wondering still,
Awestruck at these people!

Historic Guildhall, Shelburne's pride,
Could hardly get all these inside,
A Town Hall must the means provide,
For meeting which choicer gatherings fill,
Panelled by local craftsmen's skill,
Worthies of Bucks from glass instil,
And much our minds enhance.

We, the heirs of all these ages,
Taught that experience take wages,
Find while warfare bitter rages,
The future hard to face.
But strength from retrospect we gain,
The toil and sweat are not in vain,
To greater heights we shall attain,
But only through God's Grace.'

The mention of the chairmaking trade was inevitable, and one group of workers always looked on with affection were the cane workers, so it is not surprising that a traditional folk-song emerged from the early decades of this century, and is still recalled as the now elderly cane-girls mull over of the good-old-times . . . or were they?

'Wycombe Caning Girls Song

T'was in the midle of Mendy Street a charming girl I met,
She'd deep blue eyes and golden hair, and her voice was soft
    and sweet.
She blushed at me, then looked away, and never did she mind,
For underneath her arm she had, a small bundle of cane.

'refrain'

I nearly broke my heart, never wish to see her again.
That blue eyed girl with her hair in curl,
That I met with a bundle of cane.

And then we did agree to meet again on Tom Burts Hill,
To talk of happy moments past and sweeter memories still.
And talk of happy days in store, which made us sudden stop,
Would you condescend to marry a girl who works in a caning
    shop?

'refrain'

Now all young men take my advice, when to Wycombe Town
    you go,
Don't talk to pretty caning girls, or else they'll serve you so,
They'll steal away your hearts, my boys, and well they will be
    true.
Then with those blooming polishers, they'll bolt away from
    you!'

The Bodgers could not be forgotten, and in a song with words and music by Cecil Sparkes, their story was taken to the music halls of the 1920s.

'They sings lots of songs about varmers and such,
And folks in the country what never do much,
'cept diggin' up turnips and makin' of hay,
And they tells you, you ought to be thankful to they,
For sending you up all the good things they grows,
What fattens you up from your head to your toes,
But never a word do they sing about me,
Although I supports you its easy to see.

I'm Jurkins of Wycombe, High Wycombe in Bucks,
Where I lives with mi' wife and mi' fowls and mi' ducks,
And I turns up the spindles and makes all your chairs,
Aye! I guess I'm the man at the seat of affairs.

I makes chairs of all patterns and chairs of all styles,
And most of 'em travels some 'undreds of miles.
Chippendale for the ladies what like to look smart,
And good old Brown Windsor for the plain simple heart.
A chair for the wife and the mother-in-law,
I makes 'em so comfy they'll sleep and not jaw.
For newly rich, golden settees carriage hung,
And for lovers "The Grand", cast iron legs, overstrung.

I'm Jurkins of Wycombe, High Wycombe in Bucks,
Where I lives with mi' wife and mi' fowls and mi' ducks,
And I turn up the spindles and makes all your chairs,
Aye! I guess I'm the man at the seat of affairs.
And whether you're high-born, or proud as can be,
You'd all look very "low" if it wasn't for me.'

Once the chairs were made and caned, they still had to be taken out and sold or delivered to their customers, and this was done up to the First World War by means of the horse drawn wagon loaded high with chairs. Often the men could not be paid until the wagon returned with the money paid for chairs made during the previous week. One of the drivers was Benjamin North, who started off as a papermaker and, when thrown out of work in the 1830s, turned to the furniture trade, eventually becoming a well known and respected chairmaster in the district. This extract comes from his *Autobiography,* which contains his poems and was published in 1882.

''Twas in the month of May, from Wycombe we did start,
And Monday was the day, when with our horse and cart,
We left our home to do our best,
And with the Lord we left the rest.

First day was smooth and sweet, nothing did us annoy,
For the journey was a treat, as all was peace and joy.
For all creation smiled around,
And birds did sing with cheerful sound.

Next day was not so fair, now I will tell you why,
With me it did ill fare, my horse did turn so shy,
By action he did plainly say,
"I do not mean to go this way".

In Leeds I sold my chairs, and did more orders take,
Cleared out my timber wares, and many friends did make,
My price was good, I now do tell,
Which satisfied my master well.'

Nowadays, we look back on the nineteenth and early twentieth century furniture workers with nostalgia, attributing to them a skill and expertise we often feel to be lost, and no longer present in the factories still actively working in the furniture trade of the present area. But this is not so, and in this tribute to the craftsman woodcarver Frank Hudson, I feel Harry Green in 1977 spoke of the industry as a whole.

'The Craftsman.

He shares a dying race with other men,
Born to their dedication,
That are a law unto themselves.
Who use their hands to shape and mould
The inbred skill and rhythm
Of a craft.
Taking a lifetime to learn
And making them rare
Among workers managed by machines.

With blacksmith-made tools
He gouges, chisels and carves
The pedigrees of tables and chairs
Sat at and on by Kings and Queens
And other of lesser nobility.
Figuring the attitude of grain
To a perfected completion.
Recreating the beauty of antiquity
With a singleness of purpose
Befitting the supreme aspect
Of a true craftsman.'

All Saints Parish Church interior, looking west c1930.

75

ABOVE: All Saints Parish Church, Armistice Service 1918;
BELOW: spectators standing against old church wall c1910.

ABOVE: Oakley Memorial Hall, Castle Street; BELOW: All Saints
Parish Church South Porch c1860.

ABOVE: All Saints Parish Church 1862; BELOW: The Guildhall 1863.

ABOVE: National Schools, White Hart Street 1863; BELOW:
Royal Grammar School, Easton Street c1860.

OPPOSITE ABOVE: Winter in Old Wycombe c1800; BELOW: Guildhall, looking into Paul's Row c1930; ABOVE LEFT: Church Square c1930; RIGHT: Noyes Lane 1930; BELOW: cottages backing on to Noyes Lane and fronting on churchyard 1930.

ABOVE LEFT: Crooked chimney of Black Boy c1930; RIGHT: funeral of Rev Oakley proceeding up Priory Road 1906; BELOW: Black Boy Corner, prior to demolition c1930.

ABOVE: White Hart Street c1920; BELOW: White Hart Street c1930.

ABOVE: Church Street with McIlroy's c1900; BELOW: The Priory — after alterations c1930.

ABOVE: School children in Priory Road c1910; CENTRE: Priory Road Railway Bridge c1910; BELOW: Queen Square c1900.

ABOVE LEFT: Gothic House, Bull Lane; RIGHT: Crown House, Bull Lane; BELOW: Queen
Square c1890.

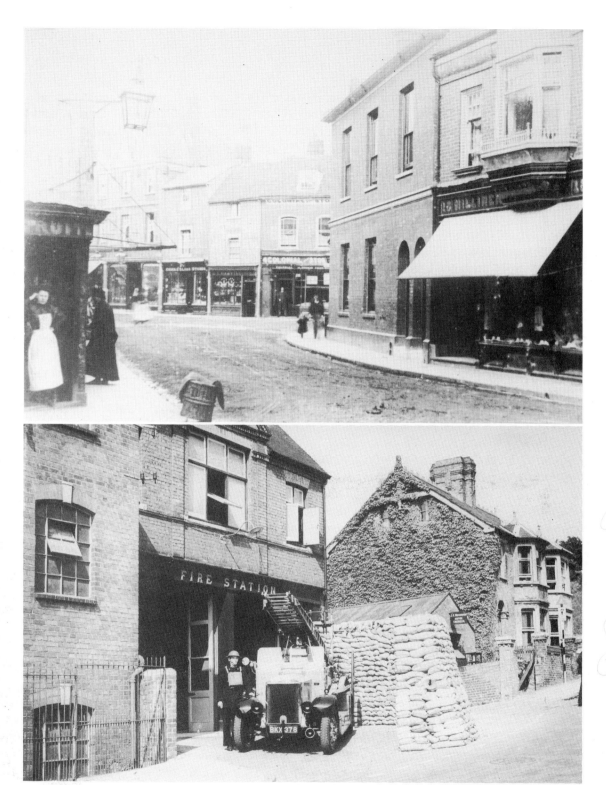

ABOVE: Queen Square c1900; BELOW: Priory Road Fire Station in the Second World War.

COMMERCIALS AND OTHERS

In this market town and industrial centre, the Councillors, Aldermen and Mayors over the past years have always been men of the town, drawn from the trades, and personally involved in the prosperity of the Borough. The early members of Parliament were also local tradesmen, and butchers certainly represented us several times in the Commons. Gradually, as the patronage of seats passed to Lord Wharton, then Lord Shelburne and Lord Carrington, politicians were drawn in to represent the Borough.

The directories of the period give us the simple details of the tradesmen of the town, but it is in the pages of publications like *High Wycombe, its resources and advantages* published in 1894, that we get to know more about the establishments·

The premier hotel in High Wycombe was the Red Lion in High Street, which 'Holds a reputation for the very highest order for civility, cleanliness and comfort, while the quality of the wines and spirits need not be discussed here, their having long ago established themselves firm favourites with connoisseurs and those who are capable of judging the merits of rare vintages'. We find that 'Commercials and others using the house can revel in the luxury of a smoke in the well-laid out garden attached . . . and the only coffee-room in the town is found here. The stabling affords accommodation for 45 horses, a fine lot of animals being owned by all jobbing purposes. The Officers of the "3rd Oxfordshire Light Infantry" trained in High Wycombe make the Red Lion their headquarters and numerous festivities are here celebrated within its walls. Mine Host is Mr. F.W. Miles, a respected native of the town, and it is the wish of all who know him that he may for many years be at hand to welcome with his genial smile and courteous attention'.

Almost opposite the Red Lion lay the Falcon Hotel, standing next to the Guildhall. This 'calls to memory the old coaching days, to those on pleasure or business bent, when away "from home", they are "at home", and Mr Bennett's greatest aim is to make his customer his guests, and make them at home. Travellers have sought the shelter of its hospitable roof long before the "iron horse" hurried its living freight into this interesting old town, but to the public no more benificial change occured, than when Mr Bennet took into his hands the reins and made the Falcon one of the most welcome places of resort in Buckinghamshire'.

The nearby Swan Hotel was managed by Mr W.K. Melsome, and, according to the guide 'One will have to travel a long way before meeting with a more comfortable or better conducted establishment. The fine clubroom is capable of holding one hundred persons, and there are also comfortable and well arranged commercial rooms and a good smoking room, and as regards the malt liquors, wines and spirits retailed in the bars, we have continually heard their praises sung'.

The commercial men who flocked to these inns came to the town to sell their wares to the retailers, and many familiar names come to mind. At this time, Messrs R. Davenport Vernon and Co were at 14 and 33 High Street, and were described as 'manufacturing and furnishing Ironmongers and cycle agents &c., &c.'; in fact the

range of goods they covered quite overwhelmed the editor of the publication: 'In attempting a brief description there is great difficulty in condensing into limited space a vast number of goods . . . which will be understood when it is mentioned that the firm issues a catalogue numbering 72 pages. The enterprise originated twenty-two years ago [1872] and since then the business has seen the establishing of the shoeing forge, van and cart works at No. 33 High Street which have worthily gained a large amount of renown. At No. 14, there are no fewer than eleven show and store rooms, not to mentioned warehouses, basement premises etc., and Mr Vernon is the honoured Captain of the Fire Brigade, is on the Executive of the National Fire Brigade Association, discharging his duties in a manner that alike deserves and receives thanks and esteem'.

Another name in the ironmongery business was Messrs Gardner and Gardner of Oxford Road and Bowdery's Lane, who included in their heading the term 'furnishing ironmongers'. Messrs Gardner 'are the sole agents for a well-known American firm dealing with chair reeds, and hold them in sizes from 11 to 42 inches in length. The firm is also noted for their chairmakers' and builders' tools and sundries; such as sofa and chair springs, glue, screws, the best French nails, webbing, chair wheel, rocking chair springs, revolving irons, and general and furnishing ironmongery of every description. Immense stocks of these goods are held, and they are continually being despatched all over the country. Mr. John William Gardner, one of the partners, is a member of the Town Council for the Eastern Ward'.

The business of builder, contractors, cabinet makers, shop fitters and furnishing undertakers was undertaken by Messrs W.R. Loosley Son & Pearce in Oxford Road; 'Such buildings as the Wycombe Grammar School in Easton Street, the Central Board School in Priory Road and Simmond's Bank in High Street, stand as evidence of the firm's skill. There are two brick kilns, one in Lane End and the other at Moor End. Funerals are conducted upon reform principles, and while every respect is paid to the deceased, due regard is had for the living'. A name linked in most people's minds with Loosley & Pearce is the establishment of Mr Thomas Hull, clothier, tailor and outfitter of Oxford Street.

'Gentlemens' youths' and boys' suits and overcoats, vests, trousers, hosiery, gloves, shirts, hats, caps, unbrellas, rugs, ties, collars, braces, waterproofs and leggings are all represented in the most comprehensive manner, mechanics clothing receives special attention, and commands a ready sale'.

To complete the wardrobe Mr John Busby was boot and shoemaker of Queen Square and Oxford Street: 'Mr Busby does a good business in the bespoke line, a great many of his customers preferring to enjoy the freedom of having their boots made to the actual size of the foot. Mr Busby is a respected member of the Corporation, has been twelve years on the School Board and is at present Chairman of the Finance Committee', and he became Mayor in 1895.

One of the oldest trades in the town was milling, and this was represented by Messrs Pearce Bros, wholesale and retail flour, corn and seed merchants of Temple Flow Mill of 114 Oxford Road, with their steam and water mills a few yards off in Bowdery's Lane: 'the firm is very old, having been established for over half a century,

originally in the very primitive little premises built principally of wood; the late Mr Job Pearce (grandfather of the present proprietor) razed it to the ground prior to building the mills as it stands today. The firm's operations extend to ten miles around; among farmers, corn merchants and seedsmen, there appears to be a great demand for their produce and specialities. There is always on hand a large stock of grain and seeds, embracing oats, maize, peas, feeding rice, flour, bran, beans, buckwheat, barley meal etc. The seeds include Canary hemp, rape, maw, millet, niger, teazle etc., also Carter's and Hyde's specialities'.

'Among the well known personages in High Wycombe is Mr. Chas Thomas Baines of W.V. Baines & Son, G.W. Railway Agents, coal merchants, and contractors for the removal and storage of furniture. The late W.V. Baines, founder of the firm, came from Windsor, where he filled the post of Station Master, dying in 1885, full of years and honours. Mr C.T. Baines was returned for the Eastern Ward in 1886 and 1892, and was made Mayor of the Borough, greatly to the satisfaction of the inhabitants. The comodious, specially constructed pantechnicon vans of the firm are amongst the most conspicuous features of High Wycombe, and are constantly being requisitioned by a superior and discriminating clientele. The horses are a particularly fine lot, their sleek well-groomed coats speaking of the care bestowed upon them'.

Also in the horse trade was Mr L. Weston, Job and Post Master and carriage builder: 'Mr Weston took up his abode in the town seventeen years ago (1877) and has the best posting business in the district. He has bought the businesses and stocks of some half-a-dozen other post masters, including Messrs Samuel Hobbs & Son, Mr A. Emmerson, and Mr Collier. The stables are close to the Railway Station and accomodate 35 horses. Mr Weston has a number of victorias, landaus, dog-carts, wagonettes, breaks and every other kind of vehicle. Large parties are catered for, and he has taken out as many as 700 pleasure seekers in one day. Mr Weston is contractor to the Post Office, and supplies horses for the local Fire Brigade. Three years ago he met a long felt public need by starting a line of buses to Loudwater and West Wycombe . . . that are thoroughly appreciated'.

A long step from the horses was the establishment of Mr H.J. Cox, hairdresser and tobacconist at the 'Lion Toilet Club' in Church Street. 'He settled here three years since [1891] and brought with him expert experience gained at a world famed establishment in Regent Street. Mr. Cox also carries on business as a tobacconist, and has a large and well-selected stock of choice tobaccos, cigars and cigarettes of the best brands.'

The firm of Messrs Rolls Brothers of 11 High Street have no doubt that 'Thanks to the Art Revival of twenty years ago, that unrelieved dullness which was characteristic of English houses a generation since, have given place to a brighter system of furnishing. The Art Movement has penetrated to every part of the country, and the firm are prepared to take a home direct from the builder, and decorate, furnish and drape it in any style the owner may require. They have published a nicely illustrated catalogue or list, showing at a glance how to furnish a house completely from £50 to £500'.

Such 'Art Furniture' would have been made by local firms such as Messrs James Cox & Son 'Art chairmakers and upholsterers'. This business was established in 1850 and, 'in addition to the home trade, Messrs Cox exports large quantities of their goods to Australia and New Zealand. Some of the designs are elaborate, while the style is artistic and reflect great credit upon the firm. Messrs Cox publish illustrated lists of their inlaid, occasional, fancy, gossip chairs, literary chairs etc., which are all made on the premises from the very best materials'.

Serving the furniture trade as a whole was Mr Jonathan Plumridge, cane chair seat manufacturer and timber merchant, steam sawing, boring and turning mills. 'Mr Plumridge began business some 28 years ago [1865] in a small way, and the business has steadily increased as the demands of the chair industry, for whom he caters, has increased. At the Desborough Road mills the work is chiefly the converting of the round timber into planks; at the Denmark Street mills, band-sawing machines are continually at work sawing the planks of wood into various parts of different pattern chairs, while two seatmaking machines are at work making cane and stuffing seats, boring lathes for boring holes in the seats, also fret-sawing machines, sawing the backs and bannisters for the better class of chairs......for the large firms of London'.

The middle of the nineteenth century was an important period in the furniture trade for High Wycombe, and a great deal of export trade was carried on, principally to Australia. The goods consisted of cane seat chairs of varied designs, and were knocked to pieces and numbered, and then packed into boxes holding three of six dozens of each. Also a large trade was done in cane seat and back folding chairs — deckchairs. The only machinery used in the town in 1850 was at the factory of the late Mr James Smith in Frogmoor, and that was of a primitive description. The class of men employed were quite different to their descendants and their living conditions were much worse. Oakmead and Desborough Road were not built on, and Temple Street, Bridge Street, Mendy Street and Denmark Street had not been long built.

After the Franco-Prussian War of 1870, a period of depression set in and lasted for some years. At this time Wycombe was known the world over as the centre for cheap chairs. Most chairs of superior class were made outside Wycombe. We had one firm of Hutchinson in St Mary Street; they turned out some beautiful work, in the shape of office chairs, cane seat and back lounge chairs, and the best class of cane seat chairs. About this time a few of the younger men of the trade began to wonder why Wycombe should not make advances in the character and quality of its commodities, and the beginning of the present high-class trade was brought about by Walter Birch, Allan Janes, James North and Charles E. Skull. In 1881, the first Furniture Exhibition was held in the Agricultural Hall in London, and Wycombe firms exhibited there. The first big firm to break away from the traditional wood low-pitched factory structure was Birch's who pulled down their old factory and dwelling house, and put up a brick factory of three storeys which had a lift and modern appliances. The greatest change to emerge was that, whereas at one time Wycombe was noted for one class of goods only, by the beginning of the 20th century, it was known in every part of the globe, as the place to buy the highest class of chairs, upholstery and cabinet work.

WONDERFUL BARGAINS

NOTICE.

POSITIVELY the LAST WEEK of BOOT SALE at BROOKS'S, White Hart Street, previous to opening at Queen Square. BOOTS at unheard-of prices to clear. It will pay you to purchase this week. Splendid line of Gents' 10/6 Boots going at 8/9, all in good condition. Football, Navvy, Men's, Women's, and Children's all at like reductions.

Note the Address -- White Hart Street.

GREAT CLEARANCE SALE.

Tremendous Sacrifice.
Wonderful Bargains.
Unheard-of Prices.

J. BUSBY

Invites the public to come and view his immense stock of

BOOTS AND SHOES

To suit all Classes, made of Good, Sound English Bark-tanned Leather, Stylish, Fashionable, and of Excellent Workmanship.

Keep your Feet Warm and Dry without Exhausting your Pocket.

Better Goods cannot be bought anywhere,
And our Prices are within the reach of all!
Pay us a Visit, & you'll go away Delighted & Happy!

ABOVE LEFT: Oliver Lockey, wine merchant, bill head 1824; RIGHT: James Lacey, advertisement; CENTRE LEFT: Brooke's Boot Sale, advertisement; RIGHT: J. Busby boots and shoes, advertisement; BELOW: Chalk's Dairy, London Road.

92

View of the Building in Hyde Park, for the Great Exhibition, 1851.

A CHALLENGE to the whole of the civilised world has been given by England, herself first among industrial nations. This challenge has been responded to from almost every quarter of the earth; and the gigantic building in which the exhibition will be held, will display specimens of man's ingenuity and perseverance, and of the great and wondrous gifts which nature has placed at his use, from every portion of the earth, into which a knowledge of the great event has penetrated.

This truly splendid structure, which is designed by Mr. Paxton, will stand on the south side of Hyde Park, and provide an exhibiting surface of 21 acres. It will be 1848 feet long, and will be crossed by a transept 108 feet high, enclosing a row of elm trees, and dividing the whole length into 948 feet on the one side, and 900 on the other. Glass and supports of iron comprise the entire structure, with the exception of timber for joists and flooring. The columns are similar throughout, and the same may be said of each of the sash-bars, and of each pane of glass. The number of columns, varying in length from 14 feet 6 inches to 20 feet, is 3,320. There are 2,284 cast-iron girders for supporting the galleries, besides 1,128 bearers or binders and 358 wrought-iron trusses for supporting the roof, 34 miles of gutters for carrying water to the columns, 202 miles of sash bars, and 900,000 superficial feet of glass. The gallery will be 24 feet wide and extend nearly a mile; and the length of table space for exhibiting will be about 8 miles. The total cubic contents of the building will be 33,000,000 feet; and the glass alone will weigh upwards of 400 tons. The total amount of contract is £79,000, the contractor retaining the materials; and the total value of the building, if it be retained by the commission, will be £150,000.

From JAMES LACEY,

Grocer, Tea Dealer & Cheesemonger,

HIGH STREET, HIGH WYCOMBE.

Teas & Coffees of the finest flavor. Home Cured Bacon, Hams, &c.

James Lacey, advertisement.

ABOVE LEFT: Brook's Boot and Shoe Stores c1910; RIGHT:
F.W. Wiles, manager of Red Lion 1893: BELOW LEFT: Dix and
Co, Church Street c1890; RIGHT: Davenport Vernon and Co
Ltd.

ABOVE LEFT: J. Busby, boot and shoe manufacturers; RIGHT:
George Welch, draper, Church Square; BELOW: Holloway and Co
Ltd, boot and shoe factory 1893.

95

ABOVE LEFT: Messrs Gardner and Gardner 1893; RIGHT: R.C. Potter, ironmonger, Cornmarket; CENTRE RIGHT: invoice of Rolls Brothers 1903; LEFT: invoice of John R. Dring 1906; BELOW RIGHT: invoice of Wheeler's Wycombe Brewery 1903.

HIGH WYCOMBE
Co-Operative Chair Manufacturing Company,
(LIMITED.)

CAPITAL £5,000, IN 5,000 SHARES OF £1 EACH.

This is to Certify that Mr. *Immanuel Wilson*

of High Wycombe Marsh is the Registered Proprietor of *Four* *Shares* in this

Company, Numbered *485. 486. 487. 488* subject to the Articles of Association, and on which the

several sums as entered on the back hereof have been paid.

Given under the Common Seal of the Company

this *seventeenth* day of *July* 1863

J. Arrowsmith Secretary.

William Avery
Amos Bridin } Directors.

No transfer of these Shares can be Registered without the production of this Certificate

ABOVE: C.O. Doel Stores c1910; BELOW: share certificate of Co-operative Chair Manufacturing Co 1863.

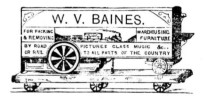
ABOVE: Webb and Fitch, advertisements 1875; **BELOW:** W.V. Baines, advertisement 1875.

98

SAMUEL HOBBS,
LIVERY & BAIT STABLES,

Red Lion Hotel,

HIGH WYCOMBE.

LICENSED TO LET

Saddle Horses, Broughams, Carriages, Waggonettes,
Dog Carts, Waggonette-Break, &c.,

FOR HIRE, BY DAY OR JOB.

RAFFETY & SON,
FURNISHING UPHOLSTERERS,

11, High Street, Wycombe.

WALNUT SUITES of DRAWING-ROOM FURNI-
TURE, in Damask, Rep, French Terry, Turkey
Cloth, Broche, Utrecht Velvet, &c., Upholstered
in a variety of styles to order.

*Common Suites in Damask or Rep, from Twelve to Nineteen Guineas;
better class Goods, from Twenty to Fifty Guineas per Suite.*

LOO and GIPSY TABLES.	GILT CORNICES and FRINGES.
OCCASIONAL TABLES.	ORNAMENTAL MANTEL BOARDS.
MUSIC CABINETS and WHATNOTS.	"DAVENPORT" WRITING DESKS.
PIER GLASSES and ORNAMENTS.	GILT GIRANDOLES.
GILT BRACKETS.	CONSOLE TABLES.

BOOKCASES, CHEFFIONEERS, WARDROBES, &c., MADE TO ORDER.

R. VERNON,
COLLIERY AGENT & COAL MERCHANT,

HIGH WYCOMBE.

ALL DESCRIPTIONS OF
HOUSE & FURNACE COAL
TO ANY STATION.

CHEAP DEPOT
FOR
BUILDING MATERIALS.

BEST AND SECOND SLATES.
STAFFORDSHIRE RIDGE TILES.
DITTO PLAIN & ORNAMENTAL PAVING.
STOURBRIDGE FIRE BRICKS.
WHITE'S INIMITABLE CEMENT.
PLASTERERS' HAIR.
TERRA COTTA CHIMNEY TOPS.
GLAZED PIPES AND CLOSET PANS.
DEALS, BATTENS, AND LATHS.

FIRE, LIFE, AND HAIL INSURANCE.

MAHOGANY, WALNUT, BIRCH, PINE, OR
JAPANNED DEAL
Bedroom Furniture.

Basin Stands, with either Marble or Wood Tops, and with
Toilet Ware to correspond in quality.

BRASS, WOOD, AND IRON BEDSTEADS
(*Either French, Arabian, Four-post, or Stump*).

A large stock of IRON BEDSTEADS, commencing at **16s.** for a full-size
French. Handsome Brass-mounted Arabian, from **75s.**

WARDROBES.	TOILETTE GLASSES.
CHESTS OF DRAWERS.	BEDROOM CHAIRS.
BASIN STANDS.	CHILDREN'S COTS.
DRESSING TABLES.	COMMODES.

*Bed Furnitures, in Chintz, Dimity, Cretonne, or Damask,
made to order.*

ABOVE LEFT: Samuel Hobbs, livery and bait stables —
advertisement 1875; **RIGHT:** R. Vernon — advertisement 1875;
BELOW: Raffety and Son — advertisement 1875.

R. DAVENPORT VERNON,

Wholesale and Retail

BUILDERS' & GENERAL IRONMONGER,

LOCKSMITH,

Bellhanger, Tin-plate Worker, &c.,

HIGH STREET, HIGH WYCOMBE.

CLOSE AND OPEN FIRE KITCHEN RANGES.

REGISTER STOVES AND CHIMNEY PIECES.

Shop, Laundry, Gas Cooking, & Petroleum Stoves.

Flavel's Improved Kitchen Ranges and Kitcheners.

Self-acting Cottage Ranges, American Cooking Stoves, Harness-Room Grates, &c.

Estimates given for supplying and fixing Ranges and Kitcheners, and old Ranges taken in Exchange.

RAIN-WATER PIPE AND GUTTERING.
PATENT, WROUGHT, AND CUT NAILS.
CORRUGATED IRON ROOFING AND ROOFING FELT.
GALVANIZED WIRE NETTING, &c.
CARPENTERS', BRICKLAYERS', & CHAIRMAKERS' TOOLS.
Special Quotations to Builders and the Trade.

JUDSON'S

PREPARATIONS FOR FAMILY USE.

SATURATED SOLUTION OF CAMPHOR.

Pure Camphor has long been known as a powerful remedial agent in Cholera, Diarrhœa, and Dysentery, but being nearly insoluble in water, is most difficult to administer. This Saturated Solution is presented in so etherial a solvent that the Camphor is volatilized as soon as it is placed in the mouth, and its action upon the body is immediate and apparent. It is easily administered—may be given to children—and will retain its virtue any length of time.—In bottles, with full directions. 1s. and 2s. each.

AROMATIC ESSENCE OF QUININE.

Is one of the most pleasant preparations of this celebrated tonic. Its value in cases of general debility, as a restorative after illness, and in the subjugation of chronic cases of Tic, Neuralgia, and Sciatica, is well known. By this preparation the dose of Quinine can be regulated with the greatest nicety, and is at the same time an economical mode of administering this costly but valuable remedy.—In bottles, 1s. and 2s. each.

CONCENTRATED ESSENCE OF JAMAICA GINGER.

This preparation contains, in a highly concentrated state, all the valuable properties of the finest Jamaica Ginger, without the addition of any other stimulant, and is especially useful in wind spasms, flatulence, colic, indigestion, and cramp.—In bottles, 1s. each.

MYRRH AND BORAX, WITH EAU DE COLOGNE.

A deliciously refreshing lotion for the mouth and gums, removing irritability and sponginess, and giving the whole structure a healthy natural colour. It may also be used as a gargle, and will be found from its astringent character to check any tendency to relaxation of the throat, and tonsilar enlargement.—In bottles, 1s. each.

THE QUEEN'S TOOTH POWDER.

This dentifrice is prepared from a recipe dispensed for many years for the late Queen Dowager, and is unrivalled for preserving and beautifying the teeth, strengthening the gums, and imparting a delicate fragrance to the breath. It also induces a healthy action of the gums, beautifies the enamel of the teeth, and arrests decay.—In boxes, 1s. each.

WILLIAM JUDSON, Pharmaceutical Chemist,

CHURCH SQUARE, WYCOMBE.

R. DAVENPORT VERNON,

LAMP & OIL DEALER,

HIGH ST., HIGH WYCOMBE.

Crystal, Paraffin, Moderator, and Benzoline Lamps,

ON THE MOST IMPROVED PRINCIPLES.

AGENT FOR THE

Silber Lamp Company and the "Queen" and "Eclipse" Burner Lamp.

A Large and Well Selected Stock

Always on Hand, at Moderate Prices.

Consumers and the trade supplied with Kerosene, Crystal, Paraffin, Benzoline, Colza, Neatsfoot, Olive, Lard, and Burning and Machinery Oils of all descriptions.

Sole Agent in this district for the sale of the new

"ALEXANDRA OIL,"

The Safest, Purest, and most Scentless Mineral Oil sold.

JUDSON'S

HORSE & CATTLE MEDICINES.

CONDITION POWDERS.

A certain and convenient alterative, and peculiarly useful when the animal is changing its coat. They also act as a tonic, improving the appetite, assisting digestion, and at the same time producing a healthy action of the skin and bowels.

PHYSIC BALLS.

This ball is kept in various strengths, and is very carefully prepared from the recipe of a celebrated veterinary surgeon. It contains corrective aromatics, for the purpose of avoiding the irritation and constipative reaction so often the result of the administration of this class of medicines.

COUGH BALLS.

A rapid cure for Coughs, Colds, and Influenza; it also relieves immediately and permanently Chronic Coughs, Broken Wind, Catarrh, &c.

CLEANSING DRINK.

A gentle and comforting laxative, adapted to the mode of treatment now recommended in these cases by the Veterinary College. The old-fashioned stimulating drench is still kept for those customers who prefer to have it.

FEVER DRINK.

The most useful medicine a stock farmer can keep. It is adapted to fever, cold, influenza, milk fever, and the earlier stages of pneumonia. In cases of emergency, before professional help can be called in, it is invaluable.

Cordial, Red Water, Astringent, Drying Drenches, and all other Medicines for Neat Cattle.

FLY POWDER.

A certain remedy to prevent the fly striking the sheep. Packed in parcels sufficient for a score of sheep. A reduction on taking a quantity.

SCAB OINTMENT.

Two kinds are kept, the blue ointment very powerful, but apt to stain the wool; and an equally strong white ointment, the most efficacious remedy for this troublesome and fatal complaint yet introduced.

DOG MEDICINES,

For Distemper, Worms, Coughs, Dysentery, &c.

Agent for Cupiss's Condition Balls, Cuff's Farmer's Friend, Driffield Oils, James's Blistering Ointment, Leeming's Essence, Elliman's Embrocation, and all other Proprietary Medicines.

WILLIAM JUDSON, Pharmaceutical Chemist,

CHURCH SQUARE, WYCOMBE.

ABOVE: R. Davenport Vernon — advertisement, 1875; BELOW: Judson's Chemist — advertisement 1875.

100

ABOVE LEFT: Miss Drewett's school — advertisement 1875; ABOVE RIGHT: R.I. Dracott — advertisement 1875; CENTRE RIGHT: Charles W. Deacon — advertisement 1875; BELOW LEFT: F. Cross Dairy c1920; BELOW RIGHT: horse'bus passing Parish Church c1890.

SECOND NOTICE OF
Turnpike Tolls to be Let,
READING & HATFIELD TURNPIKE ROAD.

WHEREAS the tolls arising at the several toll-gates upon the above road, known by the undermentioned names, with the side-bars adjacent thereto, have been this day, pursuant to due notice, put up to be let by Auction in the lots stated below, for one year, at the Crown Hotel at Great Marlow, in the County of Bucks, at the sums hereunder mentioned (being the sums which the said tolls produced last year), and there appearing no bidder for the same, Notice is hereby given that the said tolls will be again put up, in the same lots, to be let by auction, for the term of one year, from the hour of noon of the 7th day of November next, to the best bidders for the same, at the "Crown" Hotel, at Great Marlow, Bucks, on Saturday, the 25th day of October next, at One o'clock in the afternoon, at such sums as the majority of the Trustees then present may agree upon, and in the manner directed by the Act passed in the third year of the reign of his Majesty King George the Fourth " for regulating turnpike roads."

Whoever happens to be the best bidder for either of the lots must, at the same time, pay to the Treasurer one month in advance of the rent at which such tolls shall be let, and give security, with sufficient sureties, to the satisfaction of the Trustees of the said turnpike road, for payment of the rest of the rent by prospective monthly instalments. And no person will be allowed to bid unless he or she shall previously make a deposit of at least £20, which sum will, in case such person happen to be the best bidder, be retained by the Treasurer in part of the rent so paid in advance as aforesaid.

Dated this 20th day of September, 1873.

ROBERT A. WARD,
Solicitor, Maidenhead & Marlow,
Clerk to the Trustees.

Lots.	Names of the Gates above-mentioned.	Sums which the same produced last year.
1	Shiplake Gate, The Greenland Gate, The Bisham Gate	£700
2	The Wycombe Hill Gate, Terriers Gate, Whieldon Lane Gate, Chorley Wood Gate	£515
3	Hagden Lane Gate, Black Boy Gate, Horse Shoe Gate, Fiddle Gate	£452

ABOVE LEFT: Tolls to let, Reading and Hatfield Turnpike Road 1873; ABOVE RIGHT: coachman of Castle Hill; BELOW LEFT: first Loudwater – West Wycombe horse 'bus 1882, Mr L. Weston; BELOW RIGHT; furniture warehouse and pantechnicon of W.V. Baines and Son, 1894.

102

ABOVE: Oxford to London coach c1900; BELOW: carriage in High
Street c1890.

OLD CUSTOMS DIE HARD

For an industrial town like High Wycombe, the Factories Act of 1866 was unfair, for it provided that children between the ages of eight and thirteen should go to school during half of each day. Townspeople were even more appalled to discover in 1870, when the byelaws of the new School Board were revealed, that these stipulated that children should attend school the whole day. This, Mr Weller felt 'would be very hard on the working classes; to compel children of that age to go to school the whole time, would be a hardship which would be felt by the parents, and which would likewise tell very injuriously on the chair trade of the town. If chairmakers could not have children to work for them until they were thirteen years old, it was a question of whether they would be able to make the chairs so cheap as they now did'.

Children, as well as starting work at an early age, often did work after school in order to earn money and learn the trade. A child could earn a penny per week for chair packing. One lad starting work from 4.30 to 7.30 in the evening, recalls sometimes staying on after 7.30 to make wooden wedges. The youngsters were encouraged by the men, and while still at school would be taught to use the pole lathes and turn a windsor chair leg before they were old enough to start work. One recalls coming back after 6.30 in the evening and making up chairs at the rate of one shilling for a dozen chairs.

Soon after 1874 the farmers were up in arms about the Act to Regulate the Employment of Children in Agriculture, for it provided that no employer could employ a child under eight years of age unless he was a parent or guardian; also that no child under the age of ten should be employed in an agricultural gang, except at hay harvest, corn harvest, or the gathering of hops. Although the Parliamentary measures were obviously trying to help children, local magistrates had little sympathy for them. At Quarter Sessions in 1877, a boy of thirteen was sentenced to two months' imprisonment for stealing two loaves, and even then 'the Vice-Chairman felt the boy ought to be sent to reformatory for some years'. Similarly in 1861, George Page, 'a little fellow about twelve years of age, was charged with obtaining a half-quartern loaf of bread from the shop of Mr Edwin Mealing under false pretences. Sentenced to seven days imprisonment, he was told that if he came before the magistrates again, he would be transported'.

It was not always the child who appeared before the Magistrates. Joseph Cuntrip, chimney sweep was summoned for allowing John Crutch, 'who was under 21 years of age, to ascend the chimney of John Hall for the purpose of sweeping the same'. In 1866 James Harvey was also summoned for the same crime; 'he told the boy to take off his shoes and round frock . . . I heard the boy scraping the chimney and heard him cry in the chimney. I came down frightened and asked him what made him cry. He said he could not get up or down, the boy was up the chimney half an hour'. James Harvey was fined £2 with costs of 17s.

In 1857 the shop assistants also worked long hours; 'we would especially appeal for a shortening of the Saturday night toils. Instead of eleven o'clock which often runs into midnight and Sabbath morning before the jaded tradesmen can retire to rest, why not close at ten at the latest. Such an arrangement would be a boon in many ways, the young would have more time for mental and moral improvement; and poor families would save candle and fire and labour and expenses of the tradesmen would be economised'. In time, things changed, for in March 1879 a decision was made at a meeting of the tradesmen in the town, setting a closing time of 8 pm in the summer and 7 pm in the winter.

But ladies were changing too: in November 1907 Miss Frances Dove became the first woman councillor in the Borough. 'She has been resident in the town for eleven years and apart from her school work has taken a keen and practical interest in the affairs of the town.' This serenity was not present when Mrs Despard, one of the leaders of the Woman's Suffrage Movement, visited High Wycombe Guildhall in December 1907. 'She was constantly interrupted and told "We don't want you here" that she was unable to proceed with her speeches. Disturbance reached its climax by the discharge of sulphirretted hydrogen, the obnoxious fumes from which caused many people to get up with the intention of leaving. Eventually, in the face of continued opposition, it was decided that a private meeting should be held at Speed's Hall'.

In fact, when politics came to the fore, Wycombites were not backward in rebelling. In 1885 'a large body of liberals marched in procession to record their votes, carrying at their head a loaf of bread or a large piece of beef. This a number of Conservatives endeavoured to seize and a disturbance took place in which several persons were placed "hors de combat". Soon after five o'clock stone throwing began, the Conservative Club being the first to suffer. The whole of the ground floor windows were smashed, as were those of a number of public houses and business establishments'.

Things got worse when it was realised that Viscount Curzon, the Conservative candidate, had won the seat. Lord and Lady Curzon 'were mobbed by a party of roughs, Mr Vernon received a blow on the face, Lady Curzon was crushed by the throng. They sought refuge in Mr Spicer's yard, thence to the "Prince of Wales" Inn and to Mr C.H. Hunt's yard. Mr Hunt managed to conduct her ladyship on to a scaffold and thence down the steep railway embankment to safety, only her dress being caught and torn by the hedge. The mob, which crowded the top of the bridge and its approaches, not content with howling and hooting, threw volleys of stones at Lord and Lady Curzon . . . the train was backed to the bridge . . . and soon the besieged party got into a first class compartment and the train steamed out amid cheers and groans'.

But at heart, the people of Wycombe were not so prejudiced as that might indicate. Back in the 1850s at Christmas time, the night-watchmen and Bellman began Christmas Eve celebrations in seasonal style.

'Let us suppose it is Christmas-eve and that the three noted characters have started from the Borough Boundary in St Mary Street for their night's permabulation.

"Ding-dong" goes Smith; "Past 10 and a frosty night," calls out Brown, and Jones says, —

> "Now maids arise and make your pies
> Before it grows too late".

The worthy trio pass along Hog Lane (White Hart Street) towards the Canal (Frogmoor) and thence round by the old church tower towards the Guildhall, pausing at each authorised halting-place, using the same ceremony and repeating the same words, and woe betide them if they fail in the performance of their duty.

Arrived at the top of the High-Street, they group themselves in front of the Guildhall. The bellman advances three steps, sounds "Ding-dong", and exclaims "God save the King". Another "Ding-dong", followed by "Oh yes! Oh yes!" and then he gives out his Christmas-eve ditty, —

> Since it hath been a custom, now for many years,
> For Wycombe bellman to cry out Christmas Eve,
> And, with the ding-dong of his crying bell,
> To wish you all the merry Christmas hours,
> So I, this good night, wish you all the same,
> Just allow me, for I know you all do love good cheer,
> To wish you every joy when dawns the coming year.

The two watchmen now step forward and Brown repeats: —

> Good people of Wycombe 'tis time to prepare,
> For merry old Christmas the old Christmas fare,
> The roast beef and turkeys, puddings and pies,
> And dainties to gladden all hearts and all eyes,
> Holloo boys, halloo boys, hip hip hooray,
> For merry old Christmas and old Christmas Day.

The crowd gathers round to join in the cheers, and then some one emerges from the gateway of the Falcon, with a jug of steaming hot elderberry wine and three slices of toast with which the three heroes of the Eve refresh themselves, wishing everybody "A Merry Christmas". The crier puts his bell under his arm and departs, the watchmen start on their round for the night. The crowd quickly disperse, for suddenly the door of a public house opposite is flung open for a party of mummers. "Hey-derry-down" is marching round with a consumptive looking stump of an old besom in his hands, and saying in a monotonous voice:-

> Make room, make room,
> for me and my broom;
> I must have room,
> And I will have room.
> I'm Hey-down derry,
> Christmas comes but once a year,
> A pocket full of money, a cellar full of beer,
> Come in the Duke.

We leave the mummers to finish their play in the light of the great yule-log blazing in the hearth, for I have never yet met with anyone who remembered the words of the old Wycombe Mummers' Play, although some recollect .... it being performed'.

ABOVE: Paul's Row with the old Angel Inn c1910; BELOW: The Bridge, St Mary Street c1900.

107

ABOVE LEFT: The Admiral Napier, St Mary Street c1900; RIGHT: St Mary's Cottage, St Mary Street; BELOW: St Mary Street c1930.

ABOVE: St Mary Street c1910; BELOW: Marlow Hill, entrance to
St Mary Street c1930.

ABOVE: Lily's Walk, St Mary Street; BELOW: Newlands, showing
Police Station and mortuary, demolished 1935.

ABOVE: Newlands 1904; BELOW LEFT: Birdcage Walk,
alongside the railway from Crendon Lane c1930; RIGHT: Oxford
Road Post Office c1910.

ABOVE: Desborough Road c1920; BELOW: Desborough Road
c1910.

ABOVE: Oxford Street, looking towards the Hen and Chicken
c1910; BELOW: Oxford Street, top of Bull Lane 1932.

ABOVE and BELOW: Oxford Road c1920.

RULES.

1. That the Society be called the "HIGH WYCOMBE AND DISTRICT ANTI-COMPULSORY VACCINATION LEAGUE."

2. That the objects of the Society be to defend its members against prosecution for non-vaccination, and to advocate and uphold the principles of non-compulsion, and also to return Members to the Board of Guardians and Town Council pledged to the cause.

3. That the minimum subscription for Members shall be 2/- per annum. 1/- extra being payable by quarterly instalments for each unvaccinated child for whom protection is desired.

4. No Member shall be entitled to relief until the child has been enrolled for 6 months, or unless his subcriptions are duly paid up; he shall then be entitled to have one half of the Court fees and fines allowed on conviction before the magistrates. When a Member has been enrolled for not less than 12 months, and his subscriptions all fully paid up, he shall be entitled to the allowance of the whole of the Court fees and fines.

5. If it should be necessary, in consequence of an unexpected drain upon the funds of the Society, to call a levy upon the Members, such levy shall only be called by a General Meeting, convened by 7 days clear notice, and shall in no case exceed 1/- per Member.

6. That all monies belonging to the Society shall, at the discretion of the President, Secretary, and Treasurer, be deposited in the Wycombe Savings Bank.

7. That the Officers of the Association shall consist of a President, Vice-Presidents, Secretary, Assistant Secretary, Treasurer, and Collector; to be elected annually.

8. That the business of the Association shall be conducted by a general Committee, consisting of the Officers and 12 or more Members of the Society, to be elected annually; five to form a quorum.

9. An Annual General Meeting to be held in the month of August.

J. Freer, Printer, High Wycombe.

ABOVE: High Wycombe and District Anti-Compulsory Vaccination League, rule book; BELOW: horse and cart passing The Van in Oxford Road c1900.

St Mary Street c1890 — yesterday's children in yesterday's town.

INDEX

SUBSCRIBERS

Presentation Copies

1 The Mayor's Parlour, The Town of High Wycombe
2 The Chairman's Parlour, Wycombe District Council
3 Buckinghamshire County Council
4 High Wycombe Central Library
5 High Wycombe Chair Museum
6 Guildhall Heritage Exhibition
7 Harry Green

8 Ivan & Joyce Sparkes
9 Clive & Carolyn Birch
10 Mrs D.M. Mole
11 Mrs C. McEvoy
12 John A. Harris
13 Mrs Betty Hale
14 A.W. Sparkes
15 Ian S. Horwood
16 V.T.G. Heather
17 Bernard Clifton
18 K.C. Britnell
19 A. Silvey
20 F.R. Walters
21 Mrs Una Keen
22 Mrs J.M. Brand
23 F.C.B. Covill
24 Peter A. Darvill-Evans
25 D.P. Troutt
26 John S. Bignell
27 Mrs J. Graham
28 R. Journeaux
29 Mrs E. Taylor
30 Miss L. Dovey
31 Carol Bates
32 Mrs S. Hemsworth
33 Trevor Sharkey
34 Mrs Isabel Evans
35 A. Phillips
36 Peter Chard
37 R.B. Fisher
38 Mr & Mrs R.F. Flint
39 Victoria & Albert Museum
40 Mrs Marion Miller
41 Mrs M.C. Hillson
42 J.W. Hillson
43 F.G. Bailey
44 A.H. Briggs
45 Beryl Taylor
46 S.A. Goulborn
47 D.J. Church
48 C.D. Hayward
49 R.J. Davis
50 Mr & Mrs R. Rawlinson

51 Mr & Mrs J.M. Jenkins
52 A.B. Milne
53 Mr & Mrs Bernard Peatey
54 Arthur W. Wheeler
55 Mrs C. Carter
56 Mrs J. Loobey
57 T. McLaughlan
58 Ronald Goodearl
59 Eric J. Heath
60 J.W. Beaumont
61 V.J. Bryant
62 Mr & Mrs M. Powell
63 Michael G. McCoy
64 Mr & Mrs Alan Smith
65 Mr & Mrs J.S. Gore
66 Mr & Mrs C.E. Sparks
67 Mrs D. Short
68 Mr & Mrs J. Payne
69 M. Leeder
70 Miss M.A. Burrows
71 Neil C. Timberlake
72 Paul Eckerball
73 Barry P. Sutcliffe
74 D.C. Styles
75 D. Hole
76 John Buckle
77 Ms Joan E. Standage
78 Mrs S.G. Tinworth
79 Miss J. Smith
80 R.H. Mead
81 Clive D. Sherriff
82 B.H. Findlow
83 Mr & Mrs Ian Stone
84 Bellfield Middle School
85 Mrs J. Tully
86 George E. Rolfe
87 Cora E.B. Croxson
88 Mrs B.M. Rosier
89 Mrs Patricia Archer
90 F. Reed
91 Miss S. Hastings

92 Mrs Hilary Stephenson
93 Derek Peach
94 Mrs J. Goddard
95 R.J. Goves
96 G. Broadway
97 Antony Fuller
98 R.F.W. Jarvis
99 P.F. Wheeler
100 G. Hathaway
101 Mrs A. Hathaway
102 B.H. Baldwin
103 Mrs J. Ody
104 John Thomson
105 Mrs M. Thomas
106 R.L. Dunn
107 R. Sagar
108 S.C. Maskell
109 R. Holmes
110 P. Selenic
111 Mrs A. Woodward
112 K.F. Wright
113 Mrs E. Collins
114 E.A.T. Bellworthy
115 Graham Haines
116 Philip E. Pritchard
117 John Iremonger
118 Mrs Butler
119 R.E. Collins
120 J.G. Amor
121 C.T. George
122 Mrs Wooford
123 Mrs M. Hitchens
124 Mr & Mrs D. Williams
125 Mrs Skingley
126 Mrs J.R. Willmot
127 W. Thatcher
128 G.F. Peart
129 Dr M.G. Budden
130 M. Prue
131 Mrs G. Giles
132 Eileen M. Gunter
133 Mrs C. Hughes
134 Mrs M. Eyles
135 G.A. Blinko

136 G.A. Becket
137 N.J.B. Teesdale
138 Eric D. Britnell
139 Dennis J.D. Jones
140 Douglas Head
141 G.W. Frith
142 R.D. Menday
143 Edward F. Harman
144 Mrs W. James
145 Mrs R. Saunders
146 S.W. Boreham
147 Gilbert Bennell
148 E.G. Jarvis
149 A. Schofield
150 H.M. Srao
151 P.E. Strutt
152 P.D. Lewis
153 R.E. Mildred
154 C.A. Olds
155 B. Minett
156 L.W. Hughes
157 D.A. White
158 John Greenwood
159 Peter J. Soutar
160 Mike Nicholls
161 Gordon Allan Clark
162 Mrs M.J. D'Silva
163 Dr John Preece
164 Frederick P. Oxlade
165 Eric Powell
166 G.C. Hicks
167 Mrs B.N. Webb
168 Peter F. Ray
169 R.P. Monk
170 J.M. Jackson
171 Martin Lunnon
172 Betty Howland
173 Mrs Anne Glennerster
174 Anne V.M. Thomas
175 R.T. Coleman
176
177 T.W. Clarke
178 John Durham
179 Mrs N.M. Harvey
180 H.D. King
181 B.P. White

182 Buckinghamshire County Library
251 Buckinghamshire County Library
252 L.J. Sears
253 Mrs V. Weeks
254 Anthony Hugh Child
255 Dr H.J.E. Cox
256 B. Cartwright & Son Ltd
257 B. Cartwright & Son Ltd
258 B.G. Howell
259 Mr & Mrs D.M. Arnold
260 Roger F.S. Vere
261 Barry Gay
262 Donald Ford Murray
263 G.B. Brook
264 Hamnett Raffety
265 Ivor L. Beeks
266 Stewart Linford-Chairmaker
267 Cllr K.C. Boyd MBE TD
268 T.B. Wheeler
269 C.W. Miller

270 David Evans
271 Jim Howland
272 G.R. Woolven MBE
273 B. Cartwright & Son Ltd
274 B. Cartwright & Son Ltd
275 Peter F. Booth
276 Mrs G.A. Higgins
277 Michael F.M. Prole
278 Mrs V. Weeks
279 Ivor L. Beeks
280 Mrs K. Benson
281 Heather Darvill
282 William E. Bartlett
283 V. Rolfe
284 J.M. Hutchinson
285 Mrs M.J. Lester
286 C.J. Seabright
287 Mrs Aldred
288 Miss T.E. Vernon
289 Mr & Mrs G.R. Brand
290 Alan J. O'Neill
291 R.P. Robinson
292 A.J. Wright

293 T.R. Sims
294 Loudwater County Combined School
295 Derek Woods
296 R.A.C. & Mrs. A.B. Small
297 R.E. Curtis
298 Guinions County Combined School
299 H.A. Ives
300 Sands C. Middle School
301 Sands C. Middle School
302 Mrs D.C. Saunders
303 Bellfield Middle School
304 John Veysey
305 The Park County Middle School
306 King's Wood Middle School
307 Book Hill School
308 Micklefield C.C. School
309 Desmond Keen

310 V.S. Day
311 Mrs Noreen Talbot
312 West Wycombe C.C. School
313 Terriers Middle School
314 R.W. Banks
315 R.W. Banks
316 G.L. Kendall
317 Eric Powell
318 H.R. Harford
319 R.H. Davies
320 The Library, Royal Grammar School, High Wycombe
321 Wellesbourne School Resource Centre
322 Mrs M.J. Palfrey
323 P.A.W. Dixon
324 P.M. Sharman
325 J.W. Blanch
326 Mrs D. Allman
327 Charles Bray

Remaining names unlisted

ENDPAPERS: FRONT – LEFT: *Wycombe Sentinel* published in 1832 for Disraeli; RIGHT: *High Wycombe Advertiser* 23 September, 1896; BACK – LEFT: *Bucks News Budget* 14 May, 1926; RIGHT: Poster — Water Works and Gas Works, 19th century.

" AU REVOIR."

Our work is done. This is the *last* evening edition and will be an advance issue of our final number of all that will be on sale to-morrow (Saturday).

The present edition will appear before the sun goes down, as the sun never sets on the Union Jack that has braved the breeze of a thousand years. When we put up the shutters of the " Bucks News Budget " to-morrow, it will be with the flag flying for King and country—with good will in our hearts for all, and the fervent hope that a lasting peace may soon ensue in all industries—in all classes—in all homes within our grand and glorious Empire, and with the words of Tiny Tim ringing in our ears—*God bless us, everyone.*

This publication came into being through the ready approval and encouraging support of His Worship the Mayor, R. A. Janes, Esq., on May 5th, but now that the national news service is again re-established—the finest in the world—our task is finished and we shall retire as silently as we came ready to come into action again instantly should the need arise. We can only add what we have previously written, that, if by the production of this paper, we have been the means of conveying impartial and authentic news rapidly to the many small and distant homes throughout the county, and have relieved the tension of anxiety in the slightest degree in these times of unrest, then we feel that we have accomplished our object and fulfilled our plain and loyal duty .

In other columns will be found our record of thanks to those staunch friends who have unstintedly given their assistance in this effort for King and Country.

GEORGE ERNEST OSMOND.

H. J. COX, ESQ.—V.S.C.

We desire to express our cordial thanks—and we believe we are expressing the thanks of the fathers of the great profession we have temporarily adopted—for placing at our disposal instantly suitable premises to meet the requirements of our " Bucks News Budget " venture. No further words of ours need be passed to express our appreciation—to meet this loyal subject of the King, who fought for the flag in the South African war and again in advanced age during the Great War—is more than enough. May he always face the sun and the shadows fall behind him.

THE STRIKE

MAYOR OF WYCOMBE'S ACTION.

Council approve His Work.

Extract from the Mayor's Speech.

"The same day I approached Mr. Hayter, of Messrs. Freer & Hayter, with a view to getting out a news sheet, so as to counteract any distortion of wireless, and as a means of issuing any important local news or notices ; but unfortunately Mr. Hayter felt that he had too much on hand to be able to do it. Then Mr. Osmond came to enquire if I had any objection to his producing a news sheet, and within a few hours of my expressing approval, the first number was issued. This, I believe, was the **first** of its kind in the country."

Volunteer Buses—On the side of one London bus appears this notice : " To stop this bus wring the conductor's neck once."

MUCH INDEBTED.

We are obliged to Mr. Cyril W. Roberts, of the Wheatsheaf Photographic Studios, 2 High Street, for assisting us at a time when the service must have been a hindrance to the work of his high-class photographic business.

The premises that we occupy by the courtesy of Mr. H. J. Cox, is situated above the new Tobacco Saloon that—let history record—were opened during the Great Strike, 1926. We enjoy the same address, 2 High Street.

THE " A.B.C."   *LATE.*

Bucks News Budget

ISSUED BY THE

All British Campaign.

" PLENTY FOR ALL."

No. 11.	Friday. May 14th, 1926.	One Penny.

3 London Road,
High Wycombe,
13th May, 1926.

G. E. Osmond, Esq.,
Dear Mr. Osmond,

I am writing to express my appreciation of what I consider the great service you rendered the inhabitants of Wycombe and district by producing the " Bucks News Budget." Directly the strike was called, I approached Messrs. Freer & Hayter with a view to producing a News Sheet, but they were so busy, and there is, as you know, so much to be done besides the actual printing, to bring out even a small paper, they felt unable to undertake it.

Therefore, you cannot imagine how grateful and relieved I was, when shortly after you came to me and said you were going to produce the B.N.B. I believe it was the first of the kind in the country, I congratulate you on how it was done, and most gratefully and sincerely thank you for doing it.

Yours cordially,
R. A. JANES,
Mayor.

NOTE :—*His Worship the Mayor expressed the wish that the above letter should be published.*

The A.B.C. Bucks News Budget,
2 High Street,
High Wycombe,
13th May, 1926.

His Worship the Mayor,
R. A. Janes, Esq.,
3 London Road,
High Wycombe.
Dear Mr. Mayor,

Just at the time when I am making my arrangements to bring out the last issues of " The Bucks News Budget," and preparing to cease my activities in your midst, it was a delightful and unexpected pleasure to receive your kind appreciation of whatever small service that I have rendered to my King and Country in your ancient Borough during the period of the national stress that we have just passed through.

Let me say at once that it was your ready and encouraging approval on the morning of May the 5th that determined me to meet all obstacles to put this service into immediate effect, and though now we are about to issue the last one or two editions, I desire that you will remember that I am again at your disposal for this or any other national work at a moment's notice.

Yours very sincerely,
G. ERNEST OSMOND.

V.S.C. Registration Office,
The Guildhall,
High Wycombe,
May 14th, 1926.

The Editor,
A.B.C. " Bucks News Budget,"
2 High Street,
High Wycombe,
Dear Mr. Osmond,

Before you discontinue your A.B.C. News Budget, I should like to take this opportunity of thanking you for the help that you have given the staff of the Volunteer Service Committee and myself in the work of the registration of Volunteers.

In registering the many hundreds who gave in their names in Wycombe and district, which includes Gerrards Cross, Chalfonts, Beaconsfield, Chesham, Amersham, Gt. Missenden and Prestwood, and classifying their various trades and occupations, in addition to registering the large number of cars, motor cycles and lorries with drivers and mates for the transport of food, it entailed an enormous amount of work.

I am extremely grateful and tender my thanks and appreciation to all who so cheerfully gave me their valuable help and time in carrying on the work. Your paper has been very much appreciated by the public in supplying news during a very anxious and trying time.

Yours faithfully,
H. J. COX,
Chairman V.S.C.

Telegram received from Sir Alfred Knox, K.C.B., C.M.G., M.P.

HOUSE OF COMMONS.

Osmond, 2 High Street, High Wycombe.

Hear your News Budget is closing down and take opportunity to thank you for splendid work you have done. Your initiative has helped to defeat in Wycombe and neighbourhood the ill-advised attack upon the freedom of the Press and you deserve the thanks of all loyal citizens.

KNOX.

THE LADIES THANK POLIC[E]

The Ladies of Wycombe desire to ex[press] their gratitude to every member of [the] police force for their kind and cons[tant] watchfulness and care at all times an[d on] all occasions during the recent crisis. W[hen] on Canteen duty during the small h[ours] the chivalrous attention paid by the m[em-]bers of the force then on duty will nev[er be] forgotten.

THE MAYOR'S COFFEE CANTE[EN]

Besides the members of the Wom[en's] section of the British Legion, under [Mrs.] Backhouse, and the V.A.D.'s, under [Mrs.] Kentish, the following very kindly u[nder]took duty shifts :—Mrs. Gaydon, M[iss] Butler, Mr. and Mrs. Branch, Miss Bet[t] and Miss Ferguson (Monday) ; M[rs.] Miss Youens, Miss Pawley, Mrs. Hug[hes] Miss J. Ferguson, Miss Corner, [Miss] Partridge (from the Abbey), for Tues[day;] on Wednesday the V.A.D. furnished [the] staff ; Mrs. G. Williams, Mrs. Ve[rney] Miss P. Wood, Miss A. Clarke, the M[isses] Marjorie and Marion Edwards on Thurs[day;] Miss M. Butler, Miss T. Janes, Miss [——] Miss Benjamin, Miss Grimwood and [staff] from the Abbey on Friday ; and on S[atur-]day the V.A.D. staff.

G.W.R.—HIGH WYCOMBE.

The Stationmaster, Mr. W. Thom[as,] although far from well, has been " car[rying] on " through the crisis with wond[erful] fortitude. It will be sometime befo[re he] can take it quietly, as there is much t[o do] and it reflects the greatest credit on [him] for his staunch and untiring loyalty, [not] only to the G.W.R. Railway Company [but] to the greater company—the obliged [and] grateful population of our Town.

CHEERY POLICE APPROVAL

One of the most gratifying inci[dents] we have experienced was the kind [and] spontaneous expression of the " B[ucks] News Budget," when we were pa[ssing] down town to-day that we received [from] Constable Carrington and later from [P.C.] Cordrey. Their hearty handshakes wi[ll not] be forgotten. Other members of the [force] whose names I have not the pleasu[re of] knowing, are, I understand, similarly g[ener-]ous in their approval of our " effort," [and] until I meet them personally, I desi[re to] express my appreciation here.

THE ILLEGAL STRIKE.

Rights of Loyal Workers.

Union Payments Unlawful.

An important declaration regardin[g the] illegality of the General Strike was [made] by Mr. Justice Astbury in the Cha[ncery] Division yesterday, **in granting an in[junc-]tion restraining the branch secr[etary] and six delegates** of the Tower Hill b[ranch] of the National Sailors' and Fire[men's] Union **from calling on their mem[bers] to strike, or leave their employ[ment] without the authority of the Exec[utive] Council of the Union.**

His Lordship said the so-called ge[neral] strike by the Trade Union Congres[s was] unlawful and illegal, and those ta[king] part in it were not entitled to the [pro-]tection of the Trade Disputes [Act,] 1906. No trade unionist in the cou[ntry] could lose his benefits by refusin[g to] obey these unlawful orders, and t[hose] who did obey were not entitle[d to] strike pay.

STOP PRESS.

Railway disaffection adjusted. [Com-]pany's take men back in orde[r of] seniority and N.U.R. undertak[e not] to strike again before full negotia[tion] with Companys have been concl[uded.] It is understood that Company's [ab]sorption of re-engaged employees [must] necessarily be slow.

(Reuter[.)]

Printed by Freer & Hayter, 3 Easto[n Street,] High Wycombe, for, and published by, [George] Ernest Osmond, Administrator, All [British] Campaign, 43 Bedford Street, Strand, [Lon]don, W.C.2, and at 2 High Street, [High] Wycombe, Bucks ('phone 390).